T0333504

Towton 1461

England's bloodiest battle

Campaign • 120

Towton 1461

England's bloodiest battle

Christopher Gravett • Illustrated by Graham Turner

Series editor Lee Johnson • *Consultant editor* David G Chandler

OSPREY PUBLISHING
Bloomsbury Publishing Plc

Kemp House, Chawley Park, Cumnor Hill, Oxford OX2 9PH, UK
29 Earlsfort Terrace, Dublin 2, Ireland
1385 Broadway, 5th Floor, New York, NY 10018, USA
Email: info@ospreypublishing.com
www.ospreypublishing.com

OSPREY is a trademark of Osprey Publishing Ltd

First published in Great Britain in 2003

© Osprey Publishing Ltd, 2003

Transferred to digital print in 2010

All rights reserved. Apart from any fair dealing for the purpose of private study, research, criticism or review, as permitted under the Copyright, Designs and Patents Act, 1988, no part of this publication may be reproduced, stored in a retrieval system, or transmitted in any form or by any means, electronic, electrical, chemical, mechanical, optical, photocopying, recording or otherwise, without the prior written permission of the copyright owner. Enquiries should be addressed to the Publishers.

A catalogue record for this book is available from the British Library

ISBN: 978 1 84176 513 6

Editorial by Lee Johnson
Design by The Black Spot
Index by Alison Worthington
Maps by The Map Studio
3D bird's-eye views by The Black Spot
Battlescene artwork by Graham Turner
Originated by The Electronic Page Company, Cwmbran, UK
Printed and bound in India by Replika Press Private Ltd.

MIX
Paper from responsible sources
FSC® C016779
FSC
www.fsc.org

23 24 25 26 27 15 14 13 12 11 10

The Woodland Trust
Osprey Publishing supports the Woodland Trust, the UK's leading woodland conservation charity.

Key to military symbols

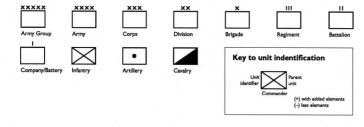

Acknowledgements
I should like to thank Moira Habberjam of the Yorkshire Archaeological Society for her unfailing assistance. I should also like to thank Malcolm Healey of the Towton Battlefield Trust and Andrew W. Boardman for sharing their experience with me. Dr Christopher Knüsel, Anthea Boylston and Veronica Fiorato of the University of Bradford kindly assisted with photographs of skeletons from the grave pit. Veronica Fiorato also read the section concerning the graves and generously offered suggestions. I am grateful to Tim Sutherland for allowing me to reproduce one of the photographs of his finds from the battlefield. Thanks are due to the staff of the Royal Armouries, including Guy Wilson, Master, who read through the manuscript and furnished yet further food for thought, Dr David Starley, Science Officer, for his insights into arrowheads including those found at Towton, Graeme Rimer, Keeper of Collections, for his comments particularly on archery and Nicholas Hall, Keeper of Artillery at Fort Nelson, for useful discussion on medieval field guns.
    Thom Richardson, Keeper of Armour and Oriental Collections, kindly provided additional photographs of the site. Graham Turner also contributed several photographs as well as his usual excellent artwork.

Artist's note
Readers may care to note that the original paintings from which the colour plates in this book were prepared are available for private sale. All reproduction copyright whatsoever is retained by the Publishers. All enquiries should be addressed to:

Graham Turner
PO Box 568
Aylesbury
Bucks
HP17 8ZX
UK

The Publishers regret that they can enter into no correspondence upon this matter.

www.ospreypublishing.com
To find out more about our authors and books visit our website. Here you will find extracts, author interviews, details of forthcoming events and the option to sign-up for our newsletter.

CONTENTS

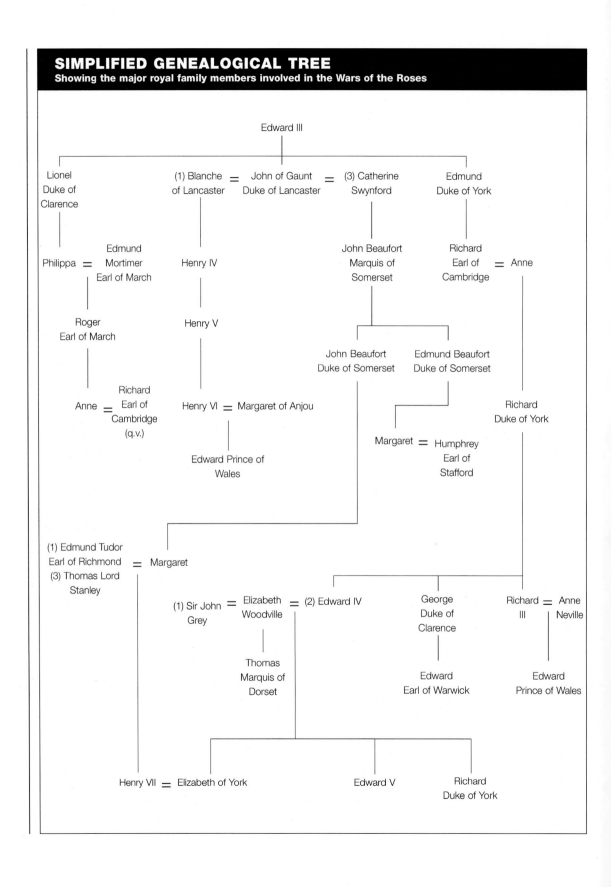

SIMPLIFIED GENEALOGICAL TREE
Showing the major royal family members involved in the Wars of the Roses

Edward III

Lionel
Duke of
Clarence

(1) Blanche = John of Gaunt = (3) Catherine
of Lancaster   Duke of Lancaster   Swynford

Edmund
Duke of York

Edmund
Philippa = Mortimer
Earl of March

Henry IV

John Beaufort
Marquis of
Somerset

Richard
Earl of = Anne
Cambridge

Roger
Earl of March

Henry V

John Beaufort
Duke of Somerset

Edmund Beaufort
Duke of Somerset

Richard
Earl of
Anne = Cambridge
(q.v.)

Henry VI = Margaret of Anjou

Richard
Duke of York

Margaret = Humphrey
Earl of
Stafford

Edward Prince of
Wales

(1) Edmund Tudor
Earl of Richmond = Margaret
(3) Thomas Lord
Stanley

(1) Sir John = Elizabeth = (2) Edward IV
Grey   Woodville

George
Duke of
Clarence

Richard = Anne
III   Neville

Thomas
Marquis of
Dorset

Edward
Earl of Warwick

Edward
Prince of Wales

Henry VII = Elizabeth of York

Edward V

Richard
Duke of York

INTRODUCTION

Portrait of Henry VI, painted in the early 16th century. (By courtesy of the National Portrait Gallery, London)

Towton has the dubious distinction of being probably the largest and bloodiest battle ever fought on English soil. Though no wholly reliable figures are available, it remains that the field was bitterly contested and resulted in substantial numbers of casualties. It marked victory for Edward IV and opened the way for his eventual coronation as King of England.

The letters of correspondents are extremely useful in giving an immediacy to the story and in conveying the flavour of the thoughts and beliefs of people at the time the events occurred. George Neville, Bishop of Exeter and Chancellor of England, was the brother of Richard Neville, Earl of Warwick (later known as 'the Kingmaker'). George wrote to Francesco Coppini, Papal Legate and Bishop of Terni in Flanders, about the 28,000 casualties at the battle of Towton. He also makes pointed comments about the Wars of the Roses generally, reflecting that such energies would have been much more usefully employed in fighting for Christianity instead, in other words in the crusades against the Turks in the East. George Neville must have had first-hand knowledge of events. Not only could he ask his brother for news (King Edward himself called him north after the battle to help settle the unrest there), George also had word from messengers and letters.

Coppini also had word from Richard Beauchamp, Bishop of Salisbury, and Nicholas O'Flanagan, Bishop of Elpin. The letters of the Bishops of Exeter and Salisbury are obviously biased in favour of the Yorkists, and Coppini was also of this persuasion. A letter from London to Pigello Portinaro, a Milanese merchant, also relates casualty figures.

These letters are in the Calendars of State Papers of Milan. Similarly the famous Paston Letters include correspondence about the battle from the Yorkist viewpoint, since the Pastons followed the Duke of Norfolk. William Paston wrote a letter on 4 April 1461, describing the receipt and contents of a letter sent by King Edward to his mother, the Duchess of York. Paston himself was able to read the letter and describes the battle itself.

Edward IV ordered an Act of Attainder to be drawn up soon after the battle of Towton, which provides a long list of names of Lancastrians attainted for treason in defying the true Yorkist king.

Chronicles put flesh on the bones of the story. John of Whethamstede, William Gregory, William Worcester and John Benet were contemporary writers but provide little additional information of value. *The Croyland Chronicle* provides a text with a Yorkist bias. *Hearne's Fragment* was written by a servant of Edward IV but relates that Towton was fought at night, something that would be virtually unique in a medieval battle. Burgundian writers may not seem to be best placed to add much to English history, but Burgundy was an ally for many years and news of this important battle appears to have reached the Continent. Philippe de Commines and Jean de Waurin can be shown to be fairly unbiased and serious historians. Waurin had done some soldiering (he fought at Agincourt in 1415) and includes information on strategy and tactics not mentioned elsewhere.

Tudor chroniclers include Polydore Vergil and Edward Hall. Vergil came to England in 1502 and proved to be a thoughtful historian. Between about 1503 and 1513 he wrote his *Polydori Vergilii Urbinatis Anglicae Historiae Libri Vigintiseptem*. Though writing under the Tudor dynasty, he produced fairly unblemished accounts of earlier reigns, using his sources carefully. Hall translated Vergil in about 1540, adding material here and there, some of which cannot be substantiated. However, both these chroniclers were writing some time after the battle, and for a pro-Lancastrian monarchy.

There is also the contemporary ballad, *The Rose of Rouen*, a Yorkist eulogy of Edward IV, who was born in Rouen. It helpfully includes a list of the Yorkist commanders at Towton.

Portrait of Edward IV painted in the early 16th century by an unknown artist but based on a portrait dateable to before 1472. (The Royal Collection © Her Majesty the Queen)

ORIGINS OF THE CAMPAIGN

The see-sawing of fortunes that marked the Wars of the Roses between the rival dynasties of York and Lancaster had their beginnings much further back. Already in the early 14th century, the deposition of Edward II as unfit had shown that the king was now increasingly thought of simply as the strongest of the nobility. This was reinforced when Richard II was removed as inadequate by Henry IV. The son of Edward III's son, John of Gaunt, Henry was, through his mother, Blanche of Lancaster, the first king of the house of Lancaster. Henry's usurpation of the throne overlooked another candidate. Roger Mortimer's father had married Philippa, daughter of Edward III's second surviving son, Lionel, Duke of Clarence, and had been heir presumptive to the unfortunate Richard II. Richard, Earl of Cambridge, descended from Edward III's fourth son, Edmund, Duke of York, married Roger's daughter, Anne, and in Henry V's reign was executed for trying to remove the king in favour of his wife's brother. When the king's own brother, Richard, Duke of York, died at Agincourt in 1415, the title passed to Richard, Earl of Cambridge's son, another Richard and the first duke of the House of York. It was not just Henry V who could trace himself back to John of Gaunt: the Beaufort dukes of Somerset, who would become key Lancastrian players in the unfolding drama, were descended from Gaunt's third marriage.

The tension rose again during the reign of Henry V's son, Henry VI. A baby when he came to the throne in 1422, even when old enough to take the reins of government Henry failed to cut the figure of a respected monarch. He never found the spirit to curb the lords, while any ambitions in France were finally extinguished in 1453 with the end

Edward, together with the Earls of Salisbury and Warwick, shown taking ship for Calais, probably after the rout of Ludford, from a manuscript of Edward's life executed in about 1470. (By permission of the British Library, Harley 7353, Picture 10)

of the Hundred Years War and the expulsion of the English (except for Calais). At home, his government was accused of poor management, and the rival faction of the House of York formed a focus for opposition.

There seems at this time to have been no real urge to remove King Henry; it was the Lancastrian courtiers whom Richard of York wanted to oust. Gradually the two sides took up arms and clashed for the first time in 1455 at St Albans. Uneasy political manoeuvring led Richard of York to suspect an attempt to crush him by Margaret of Anjou. As lords moved with their followers, Salisbury confronted a Lancastrian force on 23 September 1459 at Blore Heath, between Newcastle-under-Lyme and Market Drayton. The Yorkists held high ground, apparently against at least two cavalry charges but, despite the death of the Lancastrian Lord Audley, Salisbury had to slip away under cover of an artillery barrage. Pursued by the main Lancastrian army under King Henry, they made a stand at Ludford Bridge, only to have their gifted captain, Andrew Trollope, defect with his men on offer of pardon by the king to those who kept their faith with him. The battle became known as the rout of Ludford.

Richard, Duke of York, made for Ireland while Salisbury, Warwick and young Edward took ship for Calais. Having regrouped, they came back on 26 June 1460. Sandwich had already been seized for them and the Kentish captain, Robert Horne, came over as they advanced. They entered London and trapped Lords Scales and Hungerford in the Tower. Richard of York now arrived from Ireland. King Henry had been captured at the battle of Northampton on 10 July 1460 and conveyed, a prisoner, to London. In September Richard rode to London and at Westminster Hall he marched up to the throne and clapped his hand on it. There was an embarrassed silence from the lords present, who did not expect this overt display of ambition for the crown. Richard moved into the royal

ENGLAND, 1460–61

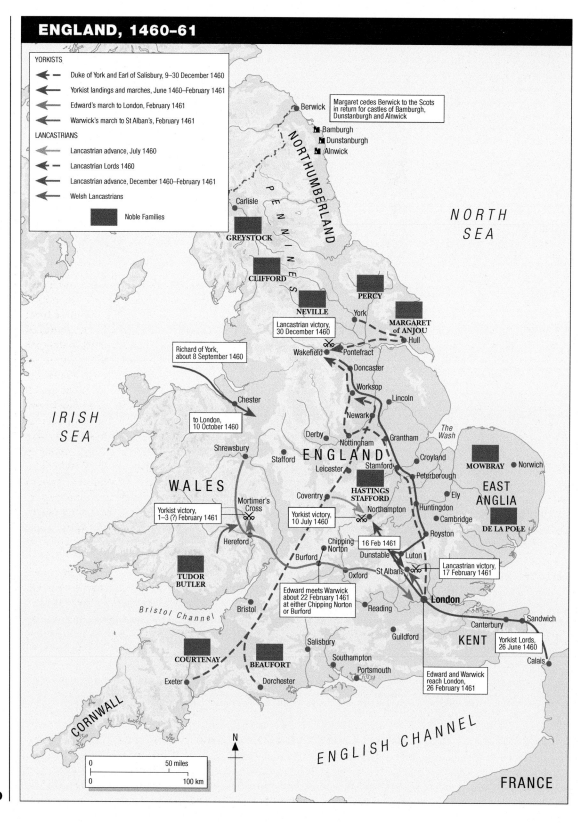

YORKISTS
- Duke of York and Earl of Salisbury, 9–30 December 1460
- Yorkist landings and marches, June 1460–February 1461
- Edward's march to London, February 1461
- Warwick's march to St Alban's, February 1461

LANCASTRIANS
- Lancastrian advance, July 1460
- Lancastrian Lords 1460
- Lancastrian advance, December 1460–February 1461
- Welsh Lancastrians

Noble Families

NORTHUMBERLAND

Berwick

Margaret cedes Berwick to the Scots in return for castles of Bamburgh, Dunstanburgh and Alnwick

Bamburgh
Dunstanburgh
Alnwick

NORTH SEA

Carlisle

GREYSTOCK

P E N N I N E S

CLIFFORD

PERCY

NEVILLE

York

Lancastrian victory, 30 December 1460

MARGARET of ANJOU

Hull

Richard of York, about 8 September 1460

Wakefield   Pontefract

Doncaster

Worksop

Chester

Lincoln

Newark

IRISH SEA

to London, 10 October 1460

Derby

Nottingham

Grantham

The Wash

Shrewsbury

Stafford

E N G L A N D

Croyland

MOWBRAY   • Norwich

Leicester

Stamford

Peterborough

WALES

Coventry

HASTINGS STAFFORD

Ely

EAST ANGLIA

Mortimer's Cross

Yorkist victory, 1–3 (?) February 1461

Yorkist victory, 10 July 1460

Northampton

Huntingdon

Cambridge

DE LA POLE

Hereford

Chipping Norton

Dunstable

Luton

Royston

Lancastrian victory, 17 February 1461

Burford

16 Feb 1461

Oxford

St Albans

TUDOR BUTLER

Edward meets Warwick about 22 February 1461 at either Chipping Norton or Burford

Reading

London

Bristol Channel

Bristol

Salisbury

Guildford

KENT

Sandwich

Canterbury

Yorkist Lords, 26 June 1460

COURTENAY

BEAUFORT

Southampton

Portsmouth

Dorchester

Calais

Exeter

Edward and Warwick reach London, 26 February 1461

CORNWALL

N

ENGLISH CHANNEL

0 — 50 miles
0 — 100 km

FRANCE

The ruins of Sandal Castle near Wakefield, to which Richard of York came with his army in December 1460. Extensive stone defences were added to the old Norman mound in the 13th century. A curious feature of the castle is the barbican added in front of the keep yet within the outer defences themselves.

apartments and a week later formerly claimed the crown through his forebear, Edward III. He now took the surname 'Plantagenet'. The nobles were not ready for this and agreed a compromise, securing a promise from the hapless King Henry that on his death Richard and his heirs would inherit the throne, and not Henry's own son, Edward. Unfortunately for the Duke of York, Henry's queen, Margaret of Anjou, had no intention of agreeing to the disinheritance of her son, and from north Wales she set about organising Lancastrian opposition in the north of England, gathering troops at York. On learning of this threat, Richard and Salisbury set out with about 5,000–6,000 men. According to William of Worcester, as they reached Worksop they came unexpectedly against troops of the Duke of Somerset, which resulted in the Yorkist vanguard receiving a mauling. On Christmas Eve they reached Sandal Castle, just south of Wakefield. Finding himself cut off, Richard sent word to his son, Edward of March, to come and relieve him. There was not enough food in the castle to feed an army, and it ran out soon after Christmas. 'Scourers' were sent out to appropriate fresh supplies. As the foraging party returned on 30 December it was attacked by elements of a Lancastrian force under the Duke of Somerset, together with the Earl of Northumberland and Lord Clifford. Seeing the prospect of much needed food about to disappear, and enemy troops close to the castle, Richard decided to lead an attack to rescue it. He may have known that Somerset was leading the opposing army, and this would undoubtedly have spurred him on. Somerset's father was an old enemy, and from this came one story that the young man deliberately lured Richard out. Hall relates how he refused to stay behind strong walls when faced by a mere queen such as Margaret! Moreover the Lancastrian army may not have appeared too large. The Yorkists charged out and aimed for the enemy force. It was only now, when it was too late, that Richard realised that this was not the entire enemy army. Another sizeable body, apparently under Somerset himself, appeared from Milnthorpe, advancing between the castle and river, cutting off escape. A Lancastrian detachment under James Butler, Earl of Wiltshire, attacked and soon seized the castle from the few men left inside, while the rest crashed into the flank of the Yorkist army. Another body may have appeared on the Yorkist right flank; as Hall says, Richard was trapped 'like a fish in a net'. It

Edward kneels before Henry VI after capturing him at the battle of Northampton on 10 July 1460. Edward carries a pollaxe, while the knight to his left, in visored sallet, has a bill. Behind him a soldier has a kettle hat whose brim is drawn down to a point over the brow. (By permission of the British Library, Harley 7353, Picture 8)

is possible that the Lancastrian divisions simply charged in as they arrived, but it seems equally likely that Somerset had deliberately split his army and left perhaps half of it concealed in the woody country beyond the castle. If so, this may have been because there was no necessity to throw the whole of his forces at a foraging party, or it may have been a deliberate lure to tempt Richard of York out of Sandal Castle. The fighting lasted, we are told, but half an hour. Despite a bitter struggle, the position was hopeless. Richard was killed and the Yorkists broke, many perishing in the nearby River Calder, others fleeing north towards Wakefield town. Richard's son, the young Earl of Rutland, was overtaken by Lord Clifford on Wakefield bridge. The Lancastrian shouted out: 'By God's blood, thy father slew mine, and so will I do thee, and all thy kin,' and ignoring pleas for mercy, stabbed the boy to death. Romanticised Victorian portraits of the scene of an unarmed and unarmoured boy being brutally murdered are not exactly true to detail, since Rutland was 17 and had obviously taken part in the fighting. The Earl of Salisbury was captured and beheaded at Pontefract by order of the Bastard of Exeter. His head, together with those of Rutland and Richard, were spiked over the gates of York. That of the latter was adorned with a paper crown in mockery of his pretensions.

The cause for the new Duke of York, Edward, seemed suddenly precarious. In Wales the Tudors were raising men in support of Queen Margaret, while she urged the northerners to march on London. A goodly number of the soldiers in the Lancastrian army were actually Scots, lured south by promises from the queen of easy plunder south of the river Trent in lieu of proper wages. They moved south, burning and pillaging as they went. Beverley was the first town to be attacked, by men of Lord Neville's contingent, 13 days after the battle of Wakefield. Not surprisingly, monastic chroniclers were quick to condemn the actions of

Plan of the battle of Wakefield. The exact positions of the troops are not known for certain.

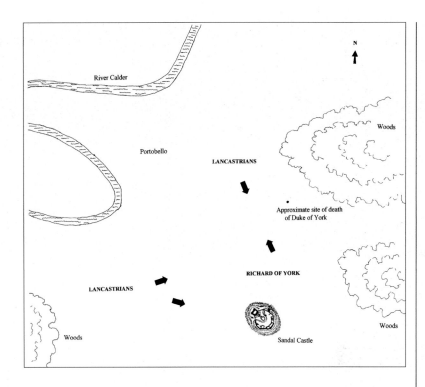

this army, especially when, as in the case of the Croyland chronicler, it affected their own religious house. He describes the contingencies put in place about the Abbey and village. Rivers or streams surrounding them were set with stakes or palisades to hinder an advance wherever the water was passable, and constant watches were set up at various points. The defences were never tested, though the Lancastrian army did pass within eight miles of the Abbey. Similarly, the Abbot of Ely hired 35 Burgundian mercenaries to protect him. Other places did suffer, however. Grantham, Stamford, Peterborough, Royston and Luton were looted. By 16 February Dunstable was invested, the defenders led, according to Gregory, by a local butcher, but no match for their opponents. Worcester says that at Dunstable Sir Edward Poyning and 200 foot were destroyed. The army swept on towards London. It was by now much smaller than when it left the north, since many natives of Scotland and the northern counties had slipped away home with their booty, though a few diehard Scots probably remained to keep their bargain with Queen Margaret.

The Earl of Warwick reached London and tried to rouse the defences, supporting the horror stories of the evil force now descending on them from the north. It was meant to drive the people of the south and midlands into a frenzy but seems to have had the opposite effect. In the atmosphere of shifting loyalties that pervaded the Wars of the Roses, a number of lords found it easier to support the allegedly stronger Lancastrians than to risk dying in opposition.

Warwick himself seems to have made no attempt to get word to Edward, now Duke of York. However, the 18-year-old prince was already capably sorting himself out. Now on the Welsh March, his first objective on learning of the demise of his father and brother was to stop the rising

The battle of Wakefield was probably fought over the open area now partly bordered by modern housing, to the right of the river. In 1460 the ground around the fields was partly wooded. This is the view from the mound at Sandal Castle, where Richard of York may have watched the Lancastrian attack on his foragers. After the battle Edward IV placed a memorial cross in what is now Manygates Lane to mark the spot where his father died. Parliamentarians destroyed it in 1645 but a new memorial, erected in 1897, survives in Manygates School. In 1825 bones, weapons, armour and other items were dug up in the area of Portobello House. Portobello is the large open area to the left of the housing.

in the west in favour of Queen Margaret. He immediately marched to confront the enemy. In the first three days of February 1461 (it is uncertain which day), he encountered the Lancastrian army led by the earls of Pembroke and Wiltshire some four miles south of Wigmore, at a place called Mortimer's Cross, where four roads met near the River Lugg. There are few details of the battle except that three suns (a parhelion) were seen in the sky. Edward took this as a good omen and afterwards added the sun in splendour to his livery badges. The Yorkists had good commanders (such as Walter Devereux, Sir William Hastings and Lord FitzWalter) and better troops, and the hasty alliance of Lancastrians and Welsh squires told against them when confronted by an enemy force with an able, vengeful, young prince at its head. The battlefield was probably cramped, set with the river on one flank and the hills on the other, and may explain one story that part of the Lancastrian army sat down; perhaps they could not take part immediately because of the packed frontage. The Yorkists won the victory, chasing the enemy south for some 16 miles, as far as Hereford. Though the earls escaped, ten other lords, including Pembroke's father, Owen Tudor, were executed in the town. Tudor's head was set up on the market cross, where a mad woman washed the blood away, combed its hair and set it about with many candles.

Meanwhile, London viewed the approaching army of Queen Margaret with suspicion, the view in the south being that it was full of northern savages (the *Croyland Chronicle* likened them to pagans or Saracens). Finally, on 12 February, the Duke of Norfolk, who had left London with his forces together with the sad figure of Henry VI, met up with the Earl of Warwick on the outskirts of St Albans in Hertfordshire. The Lancastrians had reached Dunstable, and Warwick set about ordering his defences in and around St Albans. He began setting his lines, stretching his troops in four positions from the town itself to Nomansland Common. According to Gregory, who may well have been with the Yorkist army, Warwick's dispositions were not complete when the enemy arrived on 17 February, largely it seems due to the poor quality of his scouting. He may well have had to shift his positions to meet the attack from an unexpected direction, which also entailed repositioning the defences erected by his men. Though many of the Lancastrian soldiers had gone home with their loot, perhaps 12,000 remained in the field. The second battle of St Albans began with an assault on Warwick's left flank in the town itself but his archers held their ground for a time around the watchtower, which still stands. As the Lancastrians finally fought their way through the streets they were able to assist the attack on Montagu's troops in the centre, but Warwick left the beleaguered Montagu without support for some time before bringing troops from the right. Moreover Gregory, who may have been with Warwick's division at Sandridge, commented harshly about guns firing pellets or arrows that appear to have backfired. He also notes the use of nets with nails at the knots, expanding lattices set with nails, and pavises with windows cut in them all proved to no avail in stopping the Lancastrians. Desertion by a large force of Kentish soldiers signalled the end for the Yorkists. Warwick managed to make a disciplined withdrawal, although this owed little to his generalship on the day. Edward's mother, the Duchess of York, sent her younger sons, George and Richard (the future Richard III) across the sea to the lands of England's Burgundian ally. Philip the Good, Duke of Burgundy, housed them in Utrecht. Once their brother Edward was in the ascendant they would find themselves at the ducal court in Bruges!

King Henry was reunited with Queen Margaret and, whilst at Barnet, they sent to London for food. According to *Hearne's Fragment*, the mayor and sheriffs prepared the carts but when they reached Cripplegate they were stopped by the people. The citizens were too mistrustful of the forces the queen had brought to admit them, being in 'mykel dread' of them. Learning of this attitude and of the approach of Edward and Warwick, the Lancastrian army was led back north, the troops seizing plunder on the way.

Edward had heard of Warwick's defeat when he was near Gloucester, and immediately set out for London. At Chipping Norton, or perhaps Burford, he met up with the Earl. In Edward's army were Walter Devereux, William Herbert, John Wenlock 'and many others of the Welsh Marches', recalls William Worcester. The army entered London, and Edward went to Baynard's Castle. On 1 March 1461, in the presence of the people and the army, Warwick's brother, the Chancellor George Neville, asked who should be king of England and France, to be greeted with shouts for Edward. Henry VI was denied. Two days later a council offered Edward the crown at Baynard's Castle, and on 4 March Edward was inaugurated and formally acclaimed in Westminster Abbey as King Edward IV. This had serious implications; there were now two kings in England, and a final reckoning was necessary. One of the kings would have to go.

CHRONOLOGY

1455

22 May First battle of St Albans. Drawn contest between Lancastrians and Yorkists.

1459

23 September Battle of Blore Heath. Salisbury holds off Lancastrians.
12–13 October Rout of Ludford. Yorkists defeated. Richard of York, Edward, Salisbury and Warwick escape abroad.

1460

26 June Yorkist leaders return from exile.
10 July Battle of Northampton. Henry VI captured by Yorkists.
8 September (approx) Richard of York lands to claim crown in London.
10 October Richard of York formally claims the crown.
30 December Battle of Wakefield. Richard of York and Earl of Rutland killed.

1461

1–3 February? Battle of Mortimer's Cross. Edward defeats Welsh Lancastrians.
12 February Norfolk and Warwick join forces at St Albans.
16 February Lancastrian army attacks Dunstable.
17 February Second battle of St Albans. Yorkists defeated.
26 February Edward enters London.
1 March Edward proclaimed king.
4 March Edward inaugurated as Edward IV.
5 March Norfolk leaves London to raise troops.
7 March Warwick leaves London to raise troops.
11 March Fauconberg marches from London.
12 or 13 March Edward marches from London.
22 March Edward reaches Nottingham (Jean de Waurin).
27 March (approx) Edward, Warwick and Fauconberg reach Pontefract.
28 March Battle of Ferrybridge.
29 March BATTLE OF TOWTON.
30 March Edward enters York.
22 April Edward arrives in Durham.
Early June Lancastrian attack on Carlisle beaten off by Montagu.
Late June Henry VI brought to Brancepeth by Lancastrians, chased off by Bishop of Durham.
26 June Edward arrives in London.
28 June Edward crowned in Westminster Abbey.
9 September Edward arrives at Bristol.
30 September Pembroke Castle surrenders to Herbert.

16 October Jasper Tudor, the Duke of Exeter and Welsh Lancastrians defeated at Twt Hill near Caernarfon.

1462

January Denbigh Castle surrenders to Herbert.
May Carreg Cennan Castle surrenders.
25 October Margaret and Henry VI land near Bamburgh.

1463

Early 1463 Edward returns south to Fotheringhay.
Early July Margaret, Henry VI and Scots cross border from Scotland and besiege Norham Castle.
9 December Truce with Scotland.

1464

28 March Edward marches north from London.
25 April Montagu routs Lancastrians at Hedgeley Moor.
1 May Edward marries Elizabeth Woodville at Stony Stratford.
15 May Battle of Hexham. Montagu routs the Lancastrians.
End of June Bamburgh bombarded into surrender by Yorkists.

OPPOSING COMMANDERS

Micklegate Bar, York. Over this gate were spiked the heads of Richard of York, together with those of his son, the Earl of Rutland, and the Earl of Salisbury. After the Battle of Towton Lancastrian heads graced it instead.

LEFT **The Norman Priory at Dunstable. The town lies on the old Roman Watling Street and became a target for the advancing Lancastrians in 1460. Watling Street is still a main route from the north-west to London and the south-east.**

YORKISTS

King **Edward IV** fought in a number of engagements during the Wars of the Roses. Born at Rouen in April 1442, he was nicknamed 'the Rose of Rouen'. Physically he was every inch the leader. An imposing 6ft 3½ inches tall, and at this time still of lean build, he towered over many of his contemporaries. Despite the rather pudgy portrait that has come down to us he was described as a handsome prince, with golden hair. He was physically brave and ready to lead an attack if necessary, unlike his more nervous friend, Richard, Earl of Warwick. He was ready to show mercy to a defeated foe, as in his magnanimous treatment of the Duke of Somerset in 1462 who, taken into the king's confidence, repaid it two years later with treason. This misjudgement of a powerful man may be indicative of a fatal inability on Edward's part to accurately read these powerful courtiers, and a willingness to forgive too readily. He seems to have shared this fault with his father and with his brother, the future Richard III. Generally affable and open, Edward could nevertheless present a terrifying countenance when angry, and he had a ruthless streak, necessary in a medieval commander. After the battle of Mortimer's Cross in 1461 he ordered that ten important prisoners be executed in Hereford. In the aftermath of Tewkesbury he had the Lancastrian leaders hiding in the abbey brought out and executed after a perfunctory trial. Whether sanctuary did not run to the abbey, as was implied, or whether Edward tricked the men out by safe conducts, is not known for certain. He ordered the execution of his own brother, George, Duke of Clarence, in the Tower in 1478. The repeated scheming on the part of Clarence had finally exhausted the king's patience. The quiet execution within the Tower walls indicates a strong desire on the king's part to avoid the royal family parading its dirty linen in public.

Edward was also a thinker when it came to planning strategy and tactics, and not one to panic. In the skirmishing before Towton, learning that the bridge over the river at Ferrybridge was lost, he set about outflanking the Lancastrians instead. He fought his first engagement at Northampton in July 1460, while he was still Earl of March. The Earl of Warwick was held off outside the town by entrenched Lancastrians, but Lord Grey of Ruthin betrayed them and let Edward in. He quickly used his men to roll up the Lancastrian line and so open the way for Warwick's central assault. Edward was in battle again at Mortimer's Cross in Herefordshire on about 2 February 1461, three months short of his nineteenth birthday, when he defeated the earls of Pembroke and Wiltshire. Details are sparse, but it was said that three suns were seen, which prompted Edward to assert that the Holy Trinity was watching over his army. If a true story, it demonstrates his quick thinking. His ability

The Dunstable swan jewel, found near the Priory. The swan was a badge of the Beauforts and of Henry VI, and may have been dropped by a Lancastrian supporter. It was probably made in the early 15th century, and has white enamelling, with a gold collar and chain. (British Museum, Dept of Medieval and Modern Europe, 1966, 7–3, 1)

The 15th-century watchtower in St Albans, where Yorkist archers initially held off the Lancastrian advance during the second battle of St Albans on 17 February 1461. (Photograph by Graham Turner)

would be proved again less than two months later at Towton. His use of speed won him the victory at Losecote Field near Empingham in 1470, when he defeated Sir Robert Welles before Warwick, now his enemy, could join the latter. However, Edward was not so rash to assume he could initially defeat Warwick when the latter landed in Devon, and he sailed off to Friesland rather than risk his smaller, less trustworthy forces in a battle that might easily be lost. When he returned in March 1471 he won over the city of York with claims of paternal inheritance, then moved south, gathering forces as he went. At the battles of Barnet and Tewkesbury the following year he systematically marched against, fought and routed first a Lancastrian army under Warwick, and then a second army that had landed in the west under Margaret of Anjou.

William Neville, Lord Fauconberg, proved an able commander at Towton. His energetic assault on Clifford's men at Ferrybridge and the rout afterwards suggests that Edward thought him a competent enough leader for such a task. After the manoeuvres at Ferrybridge and up the road to Towton, it was Fauconberg who had charge of the vanward, to bear the initial clash with the enemy. Described by Hall as 'a man of great policy, and of much experience in martial feats', Fauconberg is attributed by him with the idea of using the weather to advantage. He wisely kept his archers from moving within enemy range and ordered them to leave some Lancastrian arrows sticking up to hamper an enemy attack.

Richard Neville, Earl of Warwick, was a key player in the history of the time. Nicknamed 'the Kingmaker', a title whose accuracy has since been questioned, he was nevertheless a quick-witted and astute politician, and in the thick of court life, no doubt enjoying the intimacy and influence he had (or thought he had) over Edward. As a commander, however, he was not of the first rank. His strategy was defensive, not aggressive like Edward's. Even then, his shambolic defence at the second battle of St Albans, a defeat despite a whole array of defensive tricks, shows the earl's sometimes inadequate qualities of leadership in the field. Nor does he seem to have had anything like the courage that Edward demonstrated. On several occasions he appears to have become nervous when danger

This illustration of the Duke of Burgundy driven from Calais, from the *Beauchamp Pageant* of about 1480, gives an idea of fighting in the latter part of the century. A number of soldiers in the foreground and to the right wear kettle hats rather than sallets or armets, one of which is seen on a rider on the far left. Several soldiers on the right have brigandines instead of plate armour. A number of horses wear a full caparison, unusual in war at this date, plus shaffron and crinet on head and neck respectively. (By permission of the British Library, Cotton Julius E IV, Art. 6, f.24v)

threatened, for example during the surprise attack on the Yorkists at Ferrybridge. It was perhaps appropriate therefore that he should meet his end whilst attempting to escape from the battle of Barnet in 1471. By contrast, he had little sympathy for his enemies, and those men of rank unfortunate enough to be captured by him often suffered the ultimate penalty for crossing him.

John Mowbray, Duke of Norfolk, was a sick man and may not have taken part in the battle. In any case his troops arrived quite late in the day. The dukes of Norfolk could muster large retinues and knew how to use them. Under the present duke were troops led by Sir Walter Blount and the renowned Kentish captain, Robert Horne.

LANCASTRIANS

Henry Beaufort, Third Duke of Somerset, in control of the entire Lancastrian army, was only 24 years old and must have felt the eyes of the older subordinate commanders on him. He deployed his army competently, drawing up on a slight ridge awaiting a Yorkist attack, with protected flanks. He sent Clifford forward to harass the Yorkist crossing of the Aire, and proved a reasonably resourceful commander. He had successfully co-ordinated the Lancastrian assaults on the Yorkist positions at the second battle of St Albans. It was he who in 1460 had lured Edward's father into making his fatal attack at Wakefield, probably knowing that the rivalry between the two families would be useful in winkling him from Sandal Castle. If the stories are accurate, he pulled off a clever deception using part of his force to draw out the enemy while keeping other elements hidden, though this has also been attributed to Trollope. In April 1464 he almost succeeded in ambushing Lord Montagu near Newcastle, but faired less well in the following battle at Hedgeley Moor, when Percy was slain and the Lancastrian resolve broke. On 15 May Somerset picked a poor battlefield in a meadow near Hexham, the area being cramped and enclosed, with a river at his back. Many Lancastrians made off before the fight began, and Somerset paid for this piece of folly by being captured and executed.

John, Lord Clifford, showed his dash as a leader during the skirmish at Ferrybridge. He pounced on the Yorkist defenders of the bridge in the first light of a dawn raid. When he realised he was being outflanked he wasted no time in ordering a withdrawal, attempting to regain his lines. He appears to have been a man of his time, having no qualms about personally despatching the young Earl of Rutland in the blood feuds that bedevilled the politics of the day.

Henry Percy, Earl of Northumberland, commanded the van together with Andrew Trollope. Northumberland was not a quick-witted leader. It was noted at Towton that his division was slow to advance, which may have resulted in problems for him.

Perhaps one of the best commanders was **Sir Andrew Trollope** of Durham, the Master Porter, who had accompanied Edward and Salisbury from Calais on their return in 1460. It was his misfortune to find himself

The battle of Mortimer's Cross in February 1461, from an English manuscript of about 1470. Edward, centre, sees three suns in the sky, echoed below as three crowns, symbols of the Trinity. Several knights wear full armour, one carrying a pollaxe. Many other soldiers have a jacket over their body armour but wear no leg defences. To the right can be seen a (probably) simplified version of Edward's standard of the Black Bull of Clarence. (By permission of the British Library, Harley 7353, Picture 6)

The large inner bailey of Pontefract Castle. Much of the castle remains date to the 12th and 13th centuries.

set against King Henry at Ludford Bridge, and to experience a crisis of conscience that caused him to refuse to fight his sovereign. Having deserted the Yorkists during the night, he was henceforth to provide excellent service to the Duke of Somerset, but was ever after hated by the Yorkists and branded a turncoat. As a captain he was lauded by Jean de Waurin for his skill. It was perhaps Trollope who looked for novel ways to break the stalemate of armies of similar composition facing one another. He was attributed with setting the ambush that destroyed Richard, Duke of York, at Wakefield. He seems to have been behind the flank attack at the second battle of St Albans, and was afterwards knighted by Prince Edward for his valour. Trollope was an experienced soldier, but even he seems not to have realised how Fauconberg used the snowstorm to advantage against the Lancastrian archers.

OPPOSING FORCES

An impressive number of names of those who fought for the Lancastrians at Towton are preserved in the Act of Attainder passed by Edward IV after his victory (Rot. Parl. 1st Edward IV. 1461, Vol. V f.477–8)[1]. What is immediately obvious is the universal nature of the so-called Wars of the Roses. Lancastrians came to Towton from all over England and even from France and Scotland. The rather official tone of the document does not deflect from the fact that many obviously never went home again.

THE ARMIES

English armies of the 15th century consisted of two main elements: retained men and troops raised by commissions of array. Retained soldiers fought in the service of a lord, and formed the nucleus of the army. The king was the highest nobleman in the land, but there were a number of extremely powerful noblemen scattered through the country, all of which could raise their own troops, in some cases in substantial numbers. Troops were raised by contract, a mutual agreement. A lord brought a man into his service by drawing up an indenture, the latter being a parchment in which the terms of service were laid down and then repeated below. A wavy or indented line was drawn between the two sets of terms, the parchment then being cut in half along the line. One half was retained by the indentured man, the other by the lord; in case of later dispute, the two halves could be fitted together exactly. Indentured men held their own land but had to be summoned to a muster point when service was needed, which could be at any time. Some lived at such a distance that they were referred to as 'extraordinary retainers'. It was common practice for retainers to agree to serve more than one master; this was obviously more lucrative for them, but these 'well willers', as they were called, had to be careful to insert clauses into their contracts to avoid awkward situations developing if two of their masters demanded service against each other. Some followers had no contract. They were the 'feed men' who lived with their master as household retainers and had a closer bond with their lord, being given food and lodgings. They had the advantage of being ready for immediate service. As well as serving in war, duties included escorting their lord, ferrying prisoners and delivering messages. Sometimes the king gave a single contract to a leading nobleman, who sub-indented to others. Some of the retainers serving a great noble would themselves be of knightly rank, with retainers of their own. The title of esquire by this date simply meant the rank below that of knight, and many such men now bore coats-of-arms in their own right. Men who previously would have been expected to become knights had by the 15th century decided that the trappings of

[1] The relevant passage declares: 'And where also Henry Duke of Exeter, Henry Duke of Somerset, Thomas Courtenay, late Earl of Devonshire, Henry, late Earl of Northumberland, William Viscount Beaumont, Thomas Lord Roos, John, late Lord Clifford, Leo, late Lord Welles, John, late Lord Neville, Thomas Grey Knight, Lord Rugemond-Grey, Randolf, late Lord Dacre, Humphrey Dacre Knight, John Morton, late Person of Blokesworth in the shire of Dorset Clerk, Rauf Makerell, late Person of Ryesby, in the shire of Suffolk Clerk, Thomas Manning, late of New Windsor in Berkshire Clerk, John Whelpdale, late of Lichfield in the county of Stafford Clerk, John Nayler, late of London Squire, John Preston, late of Wakefield in the shire of York Priest, Philip Wentworth Knight, John Fortescue Knight, William Tailboys Knight, Edmund Moundford Knight, Thomas Tresham Knight, William Vaux Knight, Edmund Hampden Knight, Thomas Findern Knight, John Courtenay Knight, Henry Lewes Knight, Nicholas Latimer Knight, Walter Nuthill, late of Ryston in Holderness in the shire of York Squire, John Heron of the Forde Knight, Richard Tunstall Knight, Henry Bellingham Knight, Robert Whitingham Knight, John Ormond otherwise called John Butler Knight, William Mille Knight, Simon Hammes Knight, William Holand Knight called the Bastard of Exeter, William Joseph, late of London Squire, Everard Digby, late of Stokedry in the shire of Rutland Squire, John Mirfin of Southwalk in the shire of Surrey Squire, Thomas Philip, late of Dertington in Devonshire Squire, Thomas Brampton, late of Guines Squire, Giles Saintlowe, late of London Squire, Thomas Claymond, the said Thomas Tunstall Squire, Thomas Crawford, late of Calais Squire, John Audley, late of Guines Squire, John Lenche of Wich in the shire of Worcester Squire, Thomas Ormond otherwise called Thomas Butler Knight, Robert Bellingham, late of Burnalshede in the shire of Westmorland Squire, Thomas Everingham, late of Newhall in the shire of Leicester Knight, John Penycock, late of Waybridge in the county of Surrey Squire, William Grimsby, late of Grimsby in the shire of Lincoln Squire, Henry Ross, late of Rockingham in the shire of Northampton Knight, Thomas Daniel, late of Rising in the shire of Norfolk Squire, John Doubigging, late of the same Gentleman, Richard Kirkby, late of Kikby Ireleth in the shire of Lancaster Gentleman, William Ackworth, late of Luton in the shire of Bedford Squire, William Weynsford, late of London Squire, Richard Stuckley, late of Lambeth in the county of Surrey Squire, Thomas Stanley, late of Carlisle Gentleman, Thomas Litley, late of London Grocer, John Maidenwell, late of Kirton in Lindsey in the county of Lincoln Gentleman, Edward Ellesmere, late of London Squire, John Dawson, late of Westminster in the county of Middlesex Yeoman, Henry Spencer, late of the same Yeoman, John Smothing, late of York Yeoman, John Beaumont, late of Goodby in the shire of Leicester Gentleman, Henry Beaumont, late of the same Gentleman,

Roger Wharton otherwise called Roger of the Halle, late of Burgh in the shire of Westmorland Groom, John Joskin, late of Branghing in the shire of Hertford Squire, Richard Lister the younger of Wakefield Yeoman, Thomas Carr, late of Westminster Yeoman, Robert Bolling, late of Bolling in the shire of York Gentleman, Robert Hatecale, late of Barleburgh in the same shire Yeoman, Richard Everingham, late of Pontefract in the same shire Squire, Richard Fulnaby of Fulnaby in the shire of Lincoln Gentleman, Laurence Hill, late of Much Wycombe in the county of Buckingham Yeoman, Rauff Chernok, late of Thorley in the county of Lancaster Gentleman, Richard Gaitford of Estretford in Cley in the shire of Nottingham Gentleman, John Chapman, late of Wimbourne Minster in Dorset shire Yeoman, and Richard Cokerell, late of York Merchant; on Sunday called commonly Palm Sunday the 29th day of March the first year of his reign, in a field between the towns of Sherburn in Elmet and Tadcaster, in the said shire of York, called Saxtonfield and Towtonfield, in the shire of York, accompanied with Frenchmen and Scots, the Kings enemies, falsely and traitorously against their faith and liegeance, there reared war against the same King Edward, their rightwise, true, and natural liege lord, purposing there and then to have destroyed him, and deposed him of his royal estate, crown and dignity, and then and there to that intent, falsely and traitorously moved battle against his said estate, shedding therein the blood of a great number of his subjects.'

The early 19th-century bridge over the River Wharfe at Ferrybridge replaces the earlier construction over which a vicious battle was fought on 28 March 1461.

knighthood, including the expense of the ceremony and onerous public and legal duties, were not worth the title. Of similar rank to esquires were untitled gentry. Knights, squires and gentry are often termed men-at-arms; it was these men, including a lord's family members and his richer followers, who sometimes went to war encased in full plate armour. Below them in rank were the yeomen, including billmen and archers. It was the latter who often formed the largest group of a retainer's own followers.

The *Black Book* of Edward IV lists the maximum numbers of retainers expected of each rank of society; for example a duke should hold no more than 240 men; an earl 140; a knight 16. In practise the greatest lords could field far higher numbers, in some cases running to thousands of soldiers. It meant they could bring a force when summoned by the king but still have plenty in reserve. Since household feed men were not contracted it meant that numbers of soldiers do not appear on records. Musters would be sent out to retainers living away from the lord's demesne, with instructions to gather at a set date at a set place with an agreed number of men, the latter sometimes specified to be tall in stature. John Paston received such a call from the Duke of Norfolk to join the troops marching towards eventual battle at Towton, but John appears to have ignored the summons. The system was known as 'livery and maintenance' because the men maintained by the lord wore jackets in his livery colour or colours, usually the main colours of his coat-of-arms and often reflected in his standard. The greatest nobles could literally field private armies, and it became known as 'bastard feudalism'. A knight seems to have usually received 2 shillings per day, an esquire 1 shilling.

As well as retained troops, commissioners of array might be sent out to choose men for service in town and county militias, a form of recruitment favoured more by the Lancastrians. Commissions of array were usually the province of the sheriffs, but nobles also used them when it suited their purpose. Great lords actually held sway over areas technically under the county sheriff. Knights were often appointed as commissioners, to select

ABOVE **The so-called 'Leper Pot' at Barkston Ash by the A162, the base of a long lost cross shaft. (Photograph by Thom Richardson)**

LEFT **Dinting Dale, looking south along the A162 near Scarthingwell, at the junction with Saxton Lane, which leads off from the right towards Saxton village.**

the best men for service, in other words preferably the fittest and those with serviceable equipment. They were usually expected to be between the ages of 16 and 60. Where large bodies gathered they appear to have been divided into units of 1,000 and subdivided into 100s and 20s, as in the old infantry divisions. Some militias were called out by both sides, while, conversely, units might ignore the person who summoned them and go off to join the opposition. In a letter to Henry VII the mayor, aldermen and commoners of York observed that they had supplied and paid for over 1,000 men 'defensibly arrayed' to Henry VI, which had taken part in the battle of Towton, where many had been killed. They also pointed out that they had sent 400 to help the Lancastrian cause at the battle of Wakefield and a similar number at the second battle of St Albans.

Armies on both sides were thus composed of several elements. The armoured knights, esquires and gentry rode to the field but usually dismounted to fight, though mounted reserves were sometimes kept or men remounted to take part in a pursuit. Retained archers might well be horsed at this date for speed of movement, dismounting to fight. Other troops included billmen, who carried the traditional English weapon, and men with other staff weapons. The armour of these yeomen varied in quality. Militias carried a variety of armour and weapons, and most probably marched on foot. There is no mention of handgunners at Towton, nor of artillery, though the latter may have been in the train of the Duke of Norfolk and left behind *en route*.

On the march the equipment was carried in carts pulled by horses, mules or oxen. Richer men had their own wagons and these also carried their personal tents and baggage. Scouts would ride ahead to find suitable lodgings for the night, and where appropriate purchase rooms or food for the lords and their followers. When in battle formation it was usual to form three divisions, or battles, traditionally the 'van', 'vanward' or 'vaward'; the 'mainward' or 'main battle', and the 'rearward' or 'rear'. Men tended to group closely under their lord's standard, his long rallying

A 15th-century lead badge in the form of a fetterlock enclosing a rose. Both were Yorkist badges, though the fetterlock was more usually associated with the falcon. (British Museum, Dept of Medieval and Modern Europe, 56, 6–27, 116)

flag, while his square or rectangular banner with his personal heraldic arms marked him out wherever he went. Signals were given by trumpet or hand, when word of mouth was not enough. The emotions of both Lancastrians and Yorkists must have been mixed at Towton. The Lancastrians had won recent victories and were well rested, but fought without their king; the Yorkists had just trounced Lord Clifford but were tired and outnumbered.

Numbers

Exactly how many men were present at Towton will never be known for sure. The figures given by most medieval chroniclers are notoriously inaccurate, compounded here by the lack of eyewitnesses and by the fact that contemporary writers were often physically far removed from the event. William Gregory, who had fought in battle, but not at Towton, asserted in his *London Chronicle* that the Yorkists had 200,000 men in the battle, quite apart from the larger Lancastrian army. Chroniclers do comment on the large size of the armies involved and, obvious exaggerations apart, this is quite easy to believe. The stakes in this battle were enormous. Margaret and Henry needed to totally defeat Edward or else they would face the very real danger of losing their crowns. Edward needed to strike his enemies before they could win over support and become too powerful. Edward equally needed to strengthen his credibility and snuff out the old king's cause once and for all, or his position would remain unacceptable to large numbers of people. In these circumstances each wanted as many followers as possible in order to carry through their desires. A.H. Burne calculated a total for soldiers present based on the ages of those present, of the population of England and the number of men. Using this basis he came up with a figure of 75,000 men, one-fifteenth of the numbers he thought were actually available. If it is agreed that the age range of 15–40 is acceptable (and some youths and men as old as 60 were

The Old London Road as it leaves Towton village *en route* for the crossing over the River Cock and on to Tadcaster. Now a trackway, it was once the main road to Tadcaster.

found in the mass grave at Towton), then the calculation at first seems promising. But Burne probably overestimated a population figure of 3.5 million, when perhaps 2.2 million is closer. Moreover, he did not allow for those many men slaughtered in previous encounters.

Ross calculated that some 75 per cent of the adult peerage was present. Four dukes, four earls and 20 barons took part in all, and some of the richer members could field well over 3,000 men if required. Lesser men such as squires might well field 300 archers and billmen in some instances. Ross came up with a figure of 50,000 and did not discount 75,000. Using the criteria of the size of the field and the list of names in King Edward's list of attainders, Boardman concluded that a reasonable number of household and feed men would be some 20,000 on the Lancastrian side, plus about 5,000 or more raised by commissions of array and also to include any foreign mercenaries. This gives a total of about 25,000 men. The Yorkists, without Norfolk's division, perhaps started from London with some 15,000 men but by the time they reached Ferrybridge this could have risen to around 20,000 as fresh contingents joined the marching columns. It may not be on so grand a scale as the chroniclers would have liked, but it was still an impressive number of men by the standards of the time.

Armour and Weapons

The equipment of the men who fought at Towton ranged from the finest full plate armour to simple quilted protection or perhaps just civilian clothes. Those of high rank would almost certainly be clad in plate. Most of this would be of English or northern European manufacture, and covered a man from head to foot (*cap-à-pie*, as it was termed). As opposed to the major centres in northern Italy and southern Germany, we know very little of the manufacturers in England, Flanders and France. Armour was sometimes imported from northern Italy, notably Milan and Brescia. Its characteristic trait was its smooth, slightly globular appearance, the better to make weapon points slide off its surface. The Italians also favoured an enclosed helmet called an *armet*. By contrast, the armour made in southern Germany was characterised by fluting, a process that helped guide weapon points away and also strengthened the metal. The Germans preferred a sou'wester-like form of helmet called a *sallet*. In England a taller form of *sallet* was preferred to the all-enclosing Italian *armet*. A few poorer or old-fashioned knights may have appeared in armour in an earlier plainer style, worn with a 'great basinet', a large helmet, which was secured to breast and back and restricted head movement.

A war harness weighed about 25kg and this burden was spread across the whole body. By way of comparison the harness weighed less than the equipment carried by a typical modern-day infantryman. A man who wore a war harness had trained for years and, because it was made to fit him personally, he found it little encumbrance to run, lie down or mount a horse whilst wearing it. Its greatest drawback lay in the fact that body heat could not escape, especially when the helmet was in place.

English knights do not seem to have armoured their horses except for an occasional head-defence (shaffron) and perhaps a neck-defence (crinet). Often the long colourful cloth trappers were discarded in favour of decorative leather accoutrements. The war-horse, either the 'destrier' or the slightly less expensive 'courser', was a deep-chested animal bred for

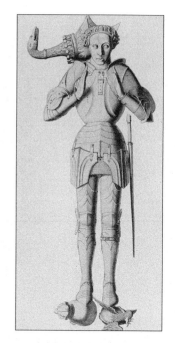

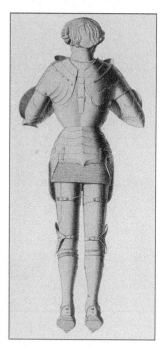

The effigy of Richard Beauchamp, Earl of Warwick, in the chapel at Warwick, as illustrated by Stothard. Though representing the Kingmaker's father-in-law, the figure wears a northern Italian armour of c.1450 of a type that could have been worn at Towton.

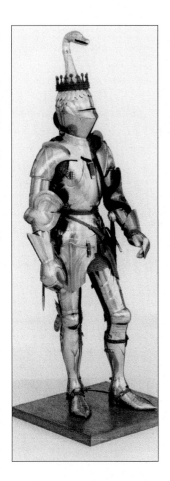

A model by Peter Wroe of a
mid-15th century northern Italian
armour based on the effigy of the
Earl of Warwick. It demonstrates
the smooth surfaces and
asymmetrical elbow-defences
that typify armour from this
area. The helmet is an *armet*.
(By courtesy of the Trustees of
the Armouries II.335)

staying power and muscle. It was not overly tall, no higher than a modern hunter, and could gallop with its armoured rider. Always a stallion, it was trained to respond to the knees and spurs, to allow its rider to use both hands if necessary. War-horses were of heavier build than the well-bred riding horses called 'palfreys'; lesser men rode 'hackneys'.

The number of fighting men who came in full plate armour would be a small percentage of the entire army. Many men who could afford at least some decent armour would equip themselves with a 'brigandine'. This was a canvas jacket lined with small pieces of plate secured by rivets, whose heads were visible on the front of the jacket. The brigandine was sometimes worn with mail sleeves, but even men of rank sometimes used them, in conjunction with plate limb defences. For those who could not afford a brigandine, the padded 'jack', made from numerous layers of quilted linen, offered good protection. Jacks and brigandines were worn by the billmen and archers, while a few may even have worn a mail shirt. In conjunction with these defences, long-tailed or short *sallets* were often worn, strapped or laced under the chin to stay in place. A few Italian deep *salades*, that look like ancient Greek helmets, might have been worn by infantry other than archers, who preferred either an open *sallet* or a simple steel cap, since these interfered least with the bowstring when drawing. A few men might have instead used a kettle-hat, rather like the British WWI-vintage helmet in appearance.

The main weapon of the knightly class was the sword, though at this date many others used it as well. Maces and war hammers were designed to stun a man, or so dent his armour that it would not function properly, while the beak on the back of the hammer was designed to punch through armour. Plate armour had made the shield virtually obsolete so, fighting on foot, both hands were free to wield a weapon. These included large hand-and-a-half swords and a variety of staff weapons including the 'pollaxe', 'halberd', 'glaive' and the *ahlespiess*, a quadrilateral spike on a haft. Sometimes daggers were used but these took second place to other weapons that had a longer reach.

Large numbers of infantrymen were archers. The longbow was as tall as a man, a self bow often made from imported Spanish yew, though elm was also occasionally used. Arrows were a clothyard long and heads varied from broad, swallow-tailed barbs, through more general purpose bullet-shaped heads with slight barbs to slim, quadrangular 'bodkins'. Arrows were bundled in sheaves, usually of 24, and carried in bags but when in battle they might be stuck in the ground to put them in easy reach.

The crossbow was never a popular battlefield weapon in late medieval England and there is little evidence for its use at Towton, except for possible skull wounds from the grave pit. There is only slight evidence for handgunners. The cannon, perhaps brought north but not used, would in all likelihood include wheeled guns mounted on split-trails for elevation. Cannonballs were at this date cut from stone, though a type of canister was also known in Europe by this date.

THE MARCH TO TOWTON

King Edward IV, the 19-year-old monarch, was keenly aware of the necessity for speed if he was to hold on to his crown. The coronation ceremony was postponed. There were more important things to be done at this time than hold imposing theatricals. The day following the proclamation, 5 March, Norfolk was sent into East Anglia to raise his forces. The Earl of Warwick set off north with a large body on Saturday 7 March to do likewise in his own lands. *Hearne's Fragment* relates that the king's footmen, largely from Wales and Kent, left on Wednesday 11 March, then noting that Edward was the last to leave. It appears that Fauconberg commanded the king's footmen, perhaps some 10,000 strong, which formed the van or lead division. According to George Neville, Norfolk, Warwick and Lord Fauconberg left London by different roads. Edward himself led out his own troops via Bishopsgate, either on the 12 March (*Hearne's Fragment*) or 13 March (George Neville). In contrast to the enemy, it is said that Edward gave strict orders that no one was to rob, commit sacrilege or rape, on penalty of death. This echoes the tight control exercised by Henry V on the road to Agincourt, but may equally have been deliberate policy to highlight the moral depravity of the Lancastrians. Nevertheless the king did secure large loans in order that his officers might procure food and lodgings *en route*, as well as to pay wages.

Edward marched up the road to St Albans and thence to Cambridge. Meanwhile the Earl of Warwick was recruiting in Coventry, where he managed to capture the Bastard of Exeter, responsible for the execution of Warwick's father, the Earl of Salisbury, after the battle of Wakefield. Not surprisingly, Exeter got short shrift at the hands of Warwick, and was himself executed. Perhaps partly in response to this event, Coventry offered 80 militia with the promise of another 40. John Benet's *Chronicle* says that Warwick then marched to Lichfield and thence towards Doncaster, where he hoped to meet up with Edward and Fauconberg, knowing that the king had passed through Newark.

Jean de Waurin states that Edward headed instead for Nottingham, where he was informed Henry VI was staying. According to the chronicler he reached the town on 22 March, only to learn that the enemy was not there; they had moved back north, across the River Aire in Yorkshire.

At some point around this time Edward must presumably have been actively seeking to join forces with Warwick and Fauconberg, rather than risk confronting the Lancastrians alone. The Duke of Norfolk, who would be late arriving at Towton itself, was even further away and could at this point offer no assistance. Despite his absence the other commanders, having united, discussed what to do next. It was decided

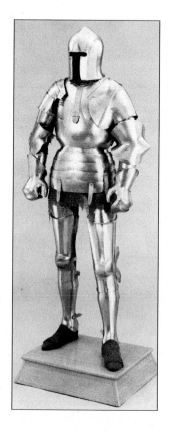

A mid-15th-century Italian armour. The helmet, a *barbute*, replaces the *armet* originally forming part of the armour. The left gauntlet is a replacement, and the tassets, culet and right elbow reinforce are missing. (Glasgow Museums: Art Gallery and Museum, Kelvingrove)

to make for the impressive Pontefract Castle (today sadly a ruin). On about 27 March the Yorkist army arrived at Pontefract. Tradition has it that they camped on a triangular piece of land below the castle on the Knottingley Road called Bubworth Heath. Here they could refresh themselves and perhaps Edward decided he could afford to wait for the troops led by Norfolk. Yet the Duke was a sick man, and the others must have wondered if he would manage the journey. Would he decide it was too much for him and simply not turn up, or possibly ignore the summons deliberately? In the climate of the times anything was possible. All that was certain was that a large enemy force lay somewhere ahead.

Having arrived at Pontefract, Edward sent ahead a force under John Radcliffe, Lord FitzWalter, to secure the crossing over the River Aire at Ferrybridge. The Lancastrians meanwhile had based themselves in the environs of the city of York, for ironically the area was quite strong in Lancastrian supporters. It is not known what their movements had been after their march back north. They may have been recruiting additional troops; commissions of array survive for York, Beverley and for some knights, which may be indicative of Lancastrian moves. Certainly large numbers of men had been arriving to swell the ranks of the army, and directions for supplying troops must have gone out once the king and queen were ensconced in the city. Once it was learned that the young Edward was marching purposefully north from London, word would have been sent out to collect the necessary soldiers for the muster in York. Men had been arriving from all over the country, even a contingent from Devon, whilst groups had even come over from Calais and also from Scotland. By the time the Lancastrian commanders decided to leave York their army was very large by the standards of the day.

An Italian *armet* of about 1450, worn with full armour of the same style. The staples along the lower edge are for securing a pierced leather strip from which hung a small mail curtain. This gave protection to the neck whilst allowing the head to turn. (By courtesy of the Trustees of the Armouries, IV.498)

It appears that King Henry, Queen Margaret and Prince Edward stayed in the city, the army being led out by the Duke of Somerset and the other commanders. As they marched out under Micklegate Bar the head of the Duke of York still remained impaled over the gate as a warning to all Yorkist sympathisers. It was said that the queen had made sure spaces were reserved over the same gate for the heads of Edward IV and the Earl of Warwick. This clear-cut humiliation of their enemies must have heartened the soldiers but some may have secretly wished that King Henry was with them at the head of his troops. Weak or not, he was still their king.

The Lancastrians moved west towards Tadcaster. From here they had to turn south to cross the River Wharfe, damaging the bridge as they did so, according to George Neville. The Old London Road then wound its way down to the smaller River Cock, which may have been in flood, and thence into the village of Towton from the north-west. The modern road enters the village from a more northerly direction. South of the village was a wide, windswept ridge. Scouts must have informed Somerset that the Yorkists were marching north to meet them, and the main Lancastrian body made camp as the commanders decided upon their choice of battlefield. The open space south of Towton was broad enough for their huge army to operate, and was the highest land in the vicinity and protected on both flanks. It was now a matter of keeping a watch for the enemy. Lord Clifford, meanwhile, was detailed to take a body of men and to move south towards the bridge over the Aire.

Brass of Sir Thomas de St Quintin, c.1445, from Harpham church in Yorkshire, showing old-style armour with a great bascinet.

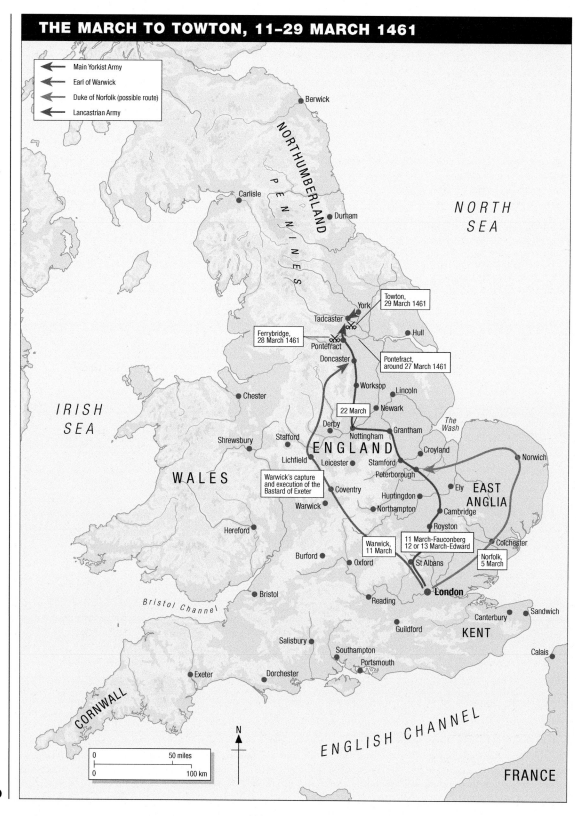

Main Yorkist Army
Earl of Warwick
Duke of Norfolk (possible route)
Lancastrian Army

NORTH
SEA

NORTHUMBERLAND

Berwick

Carlisle

Durham

P E N N I N E S

IRISH
SEA

Chester

Towton,
29 March 1461

York
Tadcaster

Hull

Ferrybridge,
28 March 1461

Pontefract

Doncaster

Pontefract,
around 27 March 1461

Worksop

Lincoln

22 March

Newark

Derby

Nottingham

Grantham

The
Wash

Shrewsbury

Stafford

E N G L A N D

Croyland

Norwich

Lichfield

Leicester

Stamford

WALES

Peterborough

EAST
ANGLIA

Warwick's capture
and execution of the
Bastard of Exeter

Coventry

Huntingdon

Ely

Warwick

Northampton

Cambridge

Hereford

Royston

Colchester

11 March–Fauconberg
12 or 13 March–Edward

Burford

Oxford

Warwick,
11 March

St Albans

Norfolk,
5 March

Bristol

Reading

London

Bristol Channel

Canterbury

Sandwich

Guildford

KENT

Salisbury

Southampton
Portsmouth

Calais

Exeter

Dorchester

CORNWALL

N

ENGLISH CHANNEL

FRANCE

0   50 miles
0   100 km

A *sallet* in northern European style from the church at Witton-le-Wear, County Durham. It is probably an export model made in northern Italy for the northern European market. (By courtesy of the Trustees of the Armouries, on loan to the Royal Armouries from the church of St Philip and St James, Witton-le-Wear)

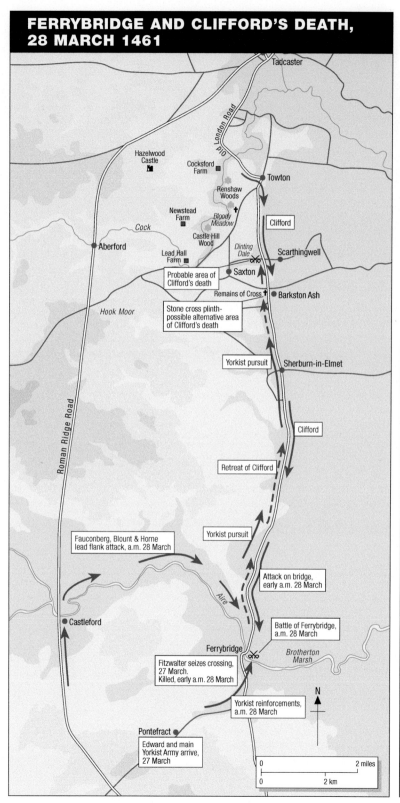

FERRYBRIDGE AND CLIFFORD'S DEATH, 28 MARCH 1461

Tadcaster

Old London Road

Hazelwood Castle

Cocksford Farm

Renshaw Woods

Towton

Clifford

Newstead Farm

Bloody Meadow

Cock

Castle Hill Wood

Dinting Dale

Scarthingwell

Aberford

Lead Hall Farm

Saxton

Probable area of Clifford's death

Remains of Cross

Barkston Ash

Stone cross plinth- possible alternative area of Clifford's death

Hook Moor

Yorkist pursuit

Sherburn-in-Elmet

Clifford

Roman Ridge Road

Retreat of Clifford

Yorkist pursuit

Fauconberg, Blount & Horne lead flank attack, a.m. 28 March

Attack on bridge, early a.m. 28 March

Aire

Castleford

Battle of Ferrybridge, a.m. 28 March

Ferrybridge

Brotherton Marsh

Fitzwalter seizes crossing, 27 March. Killed, early a.m. 28 March

N

Yorkist reinforcements, a.m. 28 March

Pontefract

Edward and main Yorkist Army arrive, 27 March

0   2 miles

0   2 km

Halberd, with a beak at the back that could pull knights from their saddles. (By courtesy of the Trustees of the Armouries, VII.)

A late 15th-century brigandine seen from the inside, showing the small iron plates which are secured to the canvas jacket by rivets. (By courtesy of the Trustees of the Armouries, III.1663)

THE BATTLE AT FERRYBRIDGE

Lord FitzWalter with a small detachment (presumably the 'foreprickers' mentioned in *Hearnes Fragment*) had seized the crossing over the Aire. The bridge itself appears to have been a wooden structure fitted with bars to enable tolls to be taken from travellers. George Neville writes that the Lancastrians had destroyed it on their way north, as an obstacle to any enemy reprisals. He says that when the Yorkist detachment arrived the enemy were on the other side. However, this seems unlikely given that he goes on to say that the Yorkists then built a 'narrow way'; hardly possible if being harassed by Clifford's men. It seems much more probable that, on finding the bridge wrecked, the Yorkists set about building a temporary wooden platform over the piles, or, less likely, a pontoon. In the early hours of Saturday 28 March (says Gregory) the men at the bridge slept, blissfully unaware that Lord Clifford – 'The Butcher' – was approaching at the head of perhaps 500 mounted men.

The Lancastrians thundered down on the river crossing, catching the sleeping guards unawares and slaughtering them before mopping up resistance. At some point FitzWalter was killed. According to Hall he died quite early on, rushing out during the initial commotion in the belief that a squabble had broken out between his soldiers. Unarmoured and carrying a pollaxe, he was soon slain. The Bastard of Salisbury, Warwick's brother, also perished. Somebody seems to have escaped and raced back to warn the Earl of Warwick, who immediately alerted Edward. Hall recounts that Warwick, mounted on a hackney, came 'blowing' to the king and, dismounting, drew his sword and thrust it into his horse, killing it, saying: 'Let him fly that will, for surely I will tarry with him that will tarry with me.'

This piece of melodrama may be something Hall invented, but if true it was an expensive demonstration of Warwick's loyalty to his men and to Edward. The king told any man who wished to depart to do so, for once committed, any who fled should be killed by the men they had betrayed, the slayers receiving remuneration and double wages. With his usual dash, the young king gathered a body of men and hurled them up the road against the Lancastrians now in possession of the bridge, while

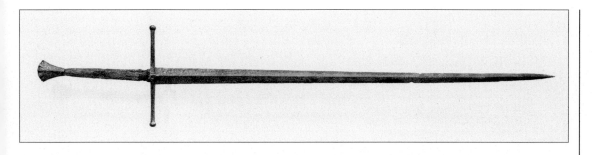

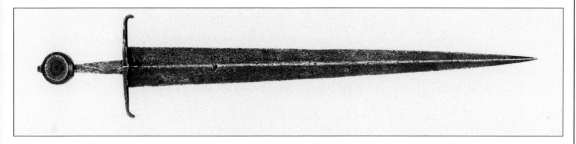

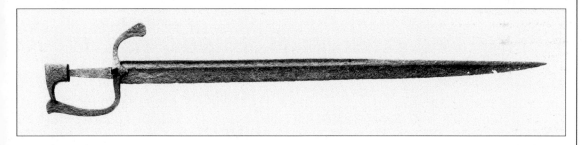

ABOVE, TOP **Sword, of hand-and-a-half form. (By courtesy of the Trustees of the Armouries, IX.)**

ABOVE, MIDDLE **An acutely pointed sword with blade of diamond-section, one of a group from the site of the English defeat at Castillon in the Dordogne in 1453. (By courtesy of the Trustees of the Armouries, IX.3683)**

ABOVE, BOTTOM **A late 15th-century hanger, a type of sword sometimes used by infantrymen. (By courtesy of the Trustees of the Armouries, IX.144)**

the rest of the Yorkist army organised itself to march out and support them. The clash, when it came, was sharp and keenly contested. Despite the large number of Yorkists now coming up the road, it was difficult to close with the Lancastrians on the narrow bridge, which Jean de Waurin says had been fortified by the Lancastrians. Backed up by their comrades on the north bank of the river, they completely halted the Yorkists, just as Clifford had planned. As men fell on both sides replacements came up. According to Gregory, Warwick was himself wounded in the leg by an arrow.

Jean de Waurin's version of events differs in several aspects. He states that Edward had reached Nottingham when he heard that the Lancastrians had taken possession of the bridge at Ferrybridge on the Friday. Edward then marched to within two miles of the enemy, which agrees with other reports of his making camp at Pontefract. He then sent John de la Pole, Duke of Suffolk, ahead with an advance party to scout the ground, but they almost ran into the enemy pickets, who were now on the south side of the river, under the command of Somerset and Earl Rivers (Lord Scales). Waurin then maintains that Edward had to send reinforcements to beat off attacks on Suffolk's men, and the Lancastrians were gradually pushed back to the bridge where they formed a defensive line. Meanwhile Edward had moved his camp closer, and coming up in person decided the bridge must be attacked quickly.

THE BATTLE AT FERRYBRIDGE (pages 34–35)

In the early hours of the morning of 28 March, Lord Clifford led a band of Lancastrians from the direction of Towton to attack the bridge over the River Aire at Ferrybridge. This had previously been broken down by the army of the Duke of Somerset to present an obstacle to Edward IV's advance, but was now in the hands of the Yorkists. Men under command of John Radcliffe, Lord FitzWalter, appear to have made some makeshift repairs, probably by planking over the supports to provide access across the bridge (1). Clifford's attack caught the Yorkists by surprise as the sentries on duty were overwhelmed, but the Lancastrians did not dislodge their enemies. Instead, a battle developed as each side refused to give way. On the north bank, retainers of Lord Clifford, distinguished by their wyvern badges (2), dismounted to oppose the Yorkists. FitzWalter was killed, but the Earl of Warwick galloped to warn King Edward, who sent additional troops forward in support of those at the bridge (3). As the new day dawned, men of Warwick's retinue, wearing their white ragged staff badges (4), fought fiercely but could not drive their enemies back. A Lancastrian knight wears plate armour in west European style, complete with a small rump-guard or *culet* plate suspended from the rear *fauld*, or skirt (5). The retainers mainly wear *sallets* (6), some fitted with visors, all held in place by a chin strap. The man behind the knight wears a mail collar of small links that form a stiff upright protection for the neck, lined for comfort and buckled at the back (7). Archers usually rode to the battlefield and so the man on the left has been able to accompany his lord on the raid (8). He wears a plain, open *sallet* so as not to impede the bowstring. The arrow thrust through his belt has the fletchings bound with twine to strengthen the glue bonding them to the shaft. The Lancastrians have chosen weapons that will not encumber them on horseback. The Lancastrian fighting at the bridge, like a number of other retainers, carries a sword and buckler (9), the latter a small fist-shield of wood and steel designed to deflect a blow or to punch an opponent. He is protected by a brigandine of small plates beneath a covering, the rivet heads visible on it's short skirt that emerges below his livery jacket (10). He also has mail sleeves and skirt, and wears long riding boots and spurs. One man carries a cavalry pennon bearing the badges of Clifford (11). Retainers of the Earl of Warwick wear similar equipment to the Lancastrians, but the leading figure carries a bill (12), while the advancing figure in plate armour wields a pollaxe (13). Behind flutter the long standards of the Earl of Warwick, rallying flags incorporating his ragged staff badge (14). (Graham Turner)

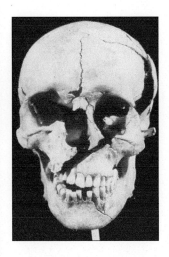

The skull of skeleton number 25 from the grave pit at Towton, an individual who was probably an archer. As well as a blade wound horizontally across the back of the head, which was probably delivered from behind as he ran, he received a massive blow from a blade diagonally across the face. This cut into the eye, nose and even the palette. (Bradford University)

Waurin notes that the bridge had been fortified by the enemy, and gives the duration of the battle as from 12.00pm to 6.00pm, during which time some 3,000 men perished in the fighting.

Edward, himself fighting on foot, soon realised that the stubborn Clifford was not going to yield this crossing easily and his tough retainers were a match for anything thrown at them. The king decided to try a different tactic, or may have initiated it before bringing up his main force. He ordered Fauconberg, Sir William Blount and Robert Horne (names supplied by Hall) to take part of the army west as far as Castleford, some three miles distant. There they crossed by the ford that gave its name to the town, and turned back along the north bank of the Aire. Now at last they could come to grips with the Lancastrians and strike them in the flank. According to Hall, when he saw this new danger, Clifford ordered the retreat and it may be that he extricated himself on seeing the enemy approaching on the north bank, before they came to grips. As they gave ground the press over the bridge became too great and they were finally pushed off it.

Fauconberg's force, which had crossed the Aire at Castleford to threaten Clifford's flank, may then have made its way north via the westerly road and thence turned right through Saxton to fall on the retreating Lancastrians as they came up the road from Ferrybridge, but it is just as likely that the Yorkists pursued them up the Towton road. Clifford's men galloped back up the road towards Sherburn-in-Elmet and thence to Towton and the waiting Lancastrian army. After them came the Yorkist horse. After a long chase they finally caught up with Clifford's men in a slight valley at a place called Dinting Dale, only some 2½ miles south of Towton. Lashing out, they brought down the enemy

RIGHT, TOP **A rondel dagger probably of the mid-15th century, from the Thames near Queenhithe, and of a form typical of the weapon sometimes carried by men-at-arms, archers or billmen. Its short reach, however, meant that it was not a primary weapon. (By courtesy of the Trustees of the Armouries, X.602)**

RIGHT, MIDDLE **A 15th-century ballock dagger. (By courtesy of the Trustees of the Armouries, X.1479)**

RIGHT, BOTTOM **A 15th-century war hammer, probably French or Italian.**

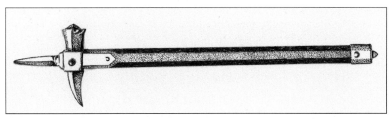

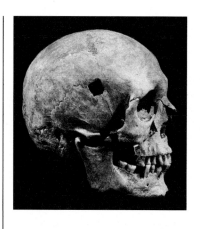

FAR LEFT **The square hole in the skull of skeleton number 9 was caused by the quadrilateral beak of a war hammer or perhaps a pollaxe. (Bradford University)**

LEFT **A late 15th-century pollaxe. The decoration denotes that it belonged to a man of means. The axe is backed by a hammer-head to concuss opponents or crack or bend armour out of shape. (By courtesy of the Trustees of the Armouries, VII.1542)**

horsemen, and here Clifford himself died, almost within reach of the main Lancastrian army. Hall, the only chronicler to describe the action at Dinting Dale, depicts the Earl as removing his gorget (a throat-defence not usually worn at this date), which Hall says he did either from heat or pain, after which an arrow, perhaps with no iron head, struck him in the throat. If the story is true, presumably mounted archers had also come up the road. Why Clifford was not backed up by Northumberland or Somerset is unknown. The unpleasant suggestion that personal jealousies may have played a role cannot be dismissed, but unless the Lancastrian army was well south of Towton, which is unlikely (Hall says their army could not see the Yorkist advance up to the southern plateau ridge the following day, suggesting the Lancastrians therefore could not be on that plateau), it simply would not have seen what was going on in the valley. However, since it is highly likely that scouts had been well forward to watch for the approaching Yorkist army, it seems reasonable to suppose that they would have seen what was happening and then reported back to their commanders. If this is the case, it may have been Somerset who, unaware of the exact strength of the enemy now approaching, decided not to intervene.

An axe said to have come from the battlefield at Towton, and now exhibited at the Duke of Northumberland's castle at Alnwick. (Collection of the Duke of Northumberland)

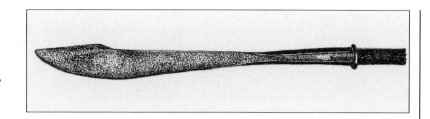

RIGHT, ABOVE **A European glaive, probably of late 15th-century date. It possesses a long convex cutting edge.**

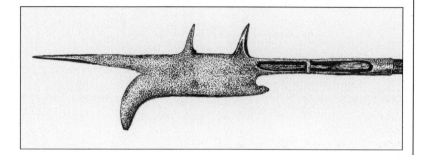

RIGHT, BELOW **A late 15th-early 16th century English bill, a form of weapon derived from the agricultural implement of the same name.**

With the bridge cleared the Yorkists began crossing the Aire. According to Waurin, the whole army passed over that same night. What happened to the dead from the battle is not known. Edward was keen to move on the enemy but must surely have allowed the bodies of FitzWalter and others of rank to be buried locally. It is recorded that a dented chalice, a spur and armour were dug up in Brotherton churchyard when preparing a grave, while C. Forrest notes that bones, armour and other relics were not infrequently found in the Brotherton Marsh along the river bank. However, as at Bosworth field, the area was the site of a later English Civil War battle, in this case in 1644, and at this remove there is no way of knowing to which conflict the items discovered belonged. Whether others were given burial in what must have been quite hard ground is open to conjecture.

The main Yorkist body now made its way forward up the same road, aware that the main Lancastrian army must lay only a few miles ahead.

THE BATTLE

As the Yorkist contingents snaked their way up the road towards Towton, they would be unable to see the Lancastrian host awaiting them, but scouts doubtless informed Edward of its whereabouts. The day was drawing to a close. Edward weighed up the situation and decided to make camp. It would take some time to order into ranks the long columns of men now coming up, and all were weary from forced marches. Many of them had just fought a hard action, some were wounded, and all no doubt wanted some food and drink in the bitter weather.

If Fauconberg's vanguard had not actually come to grips with the Lancastrians, and if the latter were chased up the road by other Yorkist bodies, Fauconberg may have moved via the Roman road to Hook Moor below Aberford, then swung north, eventually coming upon the 14th-century St Mary's church in the village of Lead, nowadays standing alone in a deserted medieval village site. The main army, however, seems to have made its way through Sherburn-in-Elmet and thence up the road to Dinting Dale, where it no doubt came upon the slaughter that had recently taken place in the area. There is no reference as to whether any of the dead were given burial, though it is hard to imagine that the corpse of a noble of Clifford's standing, hated though he might be for his violent and obstinate manner, would not be collected for burial in a local church.

But exactly where were the two armies? Waurin furnishes information that, while uncorroborated by other chroniclers, may in fact come close to the actual manoeuvring that occurred on 28/29 March 1461. After the battle of Ferrybridge, the main Yorkist army made camp north of the River Aire. On the morning of the battle, according to Waurin, Edward was advised that King Henry's army was only four miles distant, and word was brought to him that the fields were filling with armed men and banners. Edward ordered his subordinates to marshal their troops:

A ring said to have come from the battlefield at Towton. It bears a lion statant reguardant on the bezel and, in 'black-letter' on a scroll, the words Now : ys : thus. It has been associated with the 3rd Earl Percy at the battle, but the lion statant was not used by his family, nor was this motto. (British Museum, Dept of Medieval and Modern Europe, AF.771)

The earl [i.e. Edward IV] *called for his captains and told them to put their men in formation and to take their positions before the enemy came too close. And so it was he organised his battles, and he sent some men to look around the area because they were only four miles from the enemy. They did not go very far before they spotted the reconnaissance party from the enemy, and they quickly returned to the Earl of March to tell him they had seen large numbers of men at arms in the fields and the banners of King Henry. They told him how the enemy was manoeuvring and their position, and when the earl was warned of this he went to his cavalry, which he had positioned on the wing, and said to them 'My children, I pray today that we shall be good and loyal to each other because we are fighting for a good cause'.*

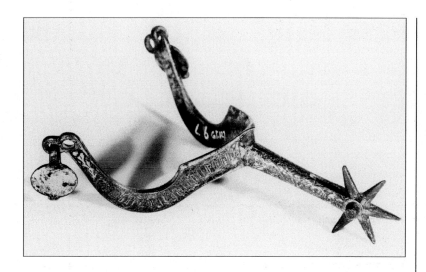

A spur said to have been found on the battlefield at Towton. The type probably dates to the early part of the 15th century and, if the provenance is accurate, shows that old-fashioned items were still used. (Society of Antiquaries)

Here is the young commander giving his pre-battle pep talk, though he appears to reserve it for the cavalry! His phrase 'My children', given to men most of whom were as old or older than he was, is interesting. It may reflect his royal bearing in considering all his subjects as his children; on the other hand it may have denoted those of his 'family', his household men. It may simply have been a canny piece of battlefield psychology – a conscious attempt to strengthen the bond between him and his men.

The passage does not make any mention of the Yorkist vanguard being much further forward. It seems to suggest that the scouts that Edward sent out were from his own troops some four miles from Towton. In that case, why did Fauconberg not send messages back from his own scouts to advise the King of the enemy positions?

Boardman has plausibly suggested the following as the most likely scenario. He believes that only the van of the Yorkist army, that is, the troops that had chased Clifford from Ferrybridge, had actually made camp in the region of Saxton and Lead, and that the main force lay further to the rear. Moreover the main body of Lancastrians were not camped around Towton but further north, nearer to Tadcaster. Both locations would signify better prospects for the lords and knights to find more comfortable accommodation: the Lancastrians in Tadcaster, the Yorkists in Sherburn-in-Elmet. Both these places are named in King Edward's Bill of Attainder issued after the battle, in the same sentence as Saxton and Towton. This emphasis given to the two main towns nearest to the battlefield may suggest a significance, perhaps as billets, before the battle. Sherburn is also four miles from Towton, which echoes Waurin's comments. If the Lancastrian main body had been camped around Tadcaster the night before the battle, it would also explain why there was no attempt to rescue Lord Clifford during the chase leading to his death.

There is high ground south-east of Saxton and to the north-west near to Lead, both areas perhaps being occupied by the Yorkist soldiers of the vanguard that streamed continually into the camps. The thick, darkening clouds betokened snow, and it must have been a cheerless night for both armies, huddled in their blankets on the hard ground

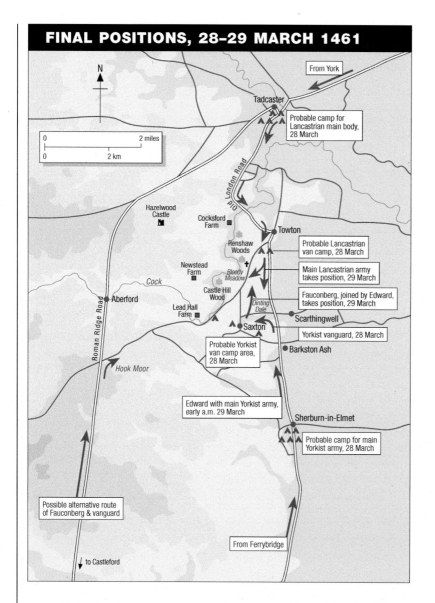

FINAL POSITIONS, 28–29 MARCH 1461

From York

Tadcaster

Probable camp for
Lancastrian main body,
28 March

0   2 miles

0   2 km

Old London Road

Hazelwood
Castle

Cocksford
Farm

Towton

Renshaw
Woods

Probable Lancastrian
van camp, 28 March

Newstead
Farm

Bloody
Meadow

Main Lancastrian army
takes position, 29 March

Cock

Castle Hill
Wood

Fauconberg, joined by Edward,
takes position, 29 March

Aberford

Lead Hall
Farm

Dinting
Dale

Scarthingwell

Saxton

Yorkist vanguard, 28 March

Roman Ridge Road

Probable Yorkist
van camp area,
28 March

Barkston Ash

Hook Moor

Edward with main Yorkist army,
early a.m. 29 March

Sherburn-in-Elmet

Probable camp for main
Yorkist army, 28 March

Possible alternative route
of Fauconberg & vanguard

From Ferrybridge

to Castleford

trying to grab a crumb of warmth and comfort amid the bleak landscape
in which they found themselves. Some of the high-born lords amongst
them may have tried sheltering in the villages, but as these probably did
not have houses of any great standing they may equally have preferred
their tents. However, these may have been with the main baggage train
with the army back at Ferrybridge, and whether any equipment would
have arrived in reasonable time is open to doubt. Lords with the main
army may have had more fortune in ordering their own tents to be
pitched. Inside they could wrap themselves in thick fur coverlets and
stand on carpets, drinking mulled wine and thinking on the morrow.
The archers, billmen and many of the poorer knightly retainers and
gentlemen had few such comforts. It is quite likely, however, that the
baggage train was well to the rear of the main army and this is suggested
by Waurin's comment that the men were short of food. Edward might

A selection of military objects found on the battlefield at Towton. These include a spur rowel and chapes from swords or daggers. (Photograph by kind permission of Tim Sutherland)

have considered his position during that bitter night, and probably said a few prayers. His army was tired and hungry, while the enemy was encamped and rested. He had nearly lost out at the bridge but was at least victorious after a hard-fought action. Yet the Lancastrian army was larger, whilst he still awaited the Duke of Norfolk.

Where was Norfolk? He may have reached Pontefract, though equally may have been well behind the rest of the Yorkist army, perhaps a day or two's march. It is possible that he was drawing artillery in his wake, but many of the field guns of the day were wheeled and light enough to be drawn by horse teams without any undue delay to the rest of the troops. It was also said that he was a sick man, and this perhaps had caused a tardiness in recruiting and perhaps also in marching. Certainly there is little evidence that he was with his troops on the day of the battle, and he would be dead within the year. Edward must have prayed he would prove loyal.

It is possible that some skirmishing took place during the night, for the vanguards of both armies were in relatively close proximity to one another and no doubt pickets were on patrol. *Hearne's Fragment* is rather strange in alleging that the battle began at 4.00pm on the Saturday, continued after dark into the next day and continued until Palm Sunday afternoon. This may be dismissed as speculation; no major medieval battles were fought at night, unless the reference should really apply to minor skirmishing the night before the battle. Alternatively, since the heavy, overcast sky would mean that darkness fell earlier than usual that Palm Sunday evening, and that some pursuit may still have been attempted at that time, *Hearne's Fragment* may have muddled up the events and days. Even so, such manoeuvres would be precarious, since horsemen chasing a broken foe would be at a distinct disadvantage in the dark, riding over unknown and perhaps broken terrain, with the chance of attack by vengeful Lancastrians who had taken refuge in woods or thickets.

Arrowheads. Broad, swallow-tailed hunting heads were designed with long cutting surfaces for severing blood vessels, and barbs to prevent their falling out. They were also highly effective against unprotected war-horses. General-purpose heads were small and sometimes had slight barbs. Some have steel coatings, presumably for use against plate armour. The quadrangular-section, armour-piercing bodkins seem to have been designed to burst mail rings apart. (By courtesy of the Trustees of the Armouries)

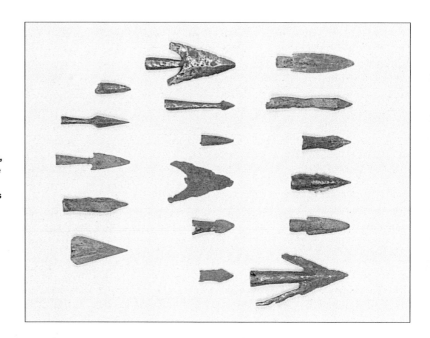

The Battlefield

Unlike so many medieval battlefields, the area over which the two armies fought is not the subject of major dispute. In his Attainders King Edward IV himself describes the battle as taking place 'in a field between the towns of Sherburn-in-Elmet and Tadcaster' and as in Saxonfield and Towtonfield. Hall states that the battle was fought between the villages of Towton and Saxton. John Leland in his *Itinerary* notes that the battle was fought as much in Saxton parish as in Towton, but bears the name of Towton. This name is also preferred by the 15th-century entry in *Hearne's Fragment,* and by Polydore Vergil. This is hardly surprising, given that the main road ran through Towton, while Saxton was a quiet village off the main highway. Other towns, more distant from the scene of a clash than is Towton in this case, have nevertheless given their names to major battles – Hastings and Bosworth are but two examples. Edward's grant to his standard bearer in 1461 describes it as the 'bataille of Sherbourne in Elmete'. Other names that predate Vergil include York Field, Palmsunday Field, and the battle of Cockbridge.

The road from Ferrybridge to Tadcaster ran northwards, climbing gently on to a broad plateau of open land beyond the Dinting Dale valley. Some have suggested that originally at Barkston Ash the road turned left to Saxton and then over the battlefield at Cotcher's Lane to Towton, but this seems an unnecessary detour. On the east the main road was flanked by marshy ground that now consists rather of water meadows. A second road from Leeds ran north-east towards the plateau, at first passing the, now deserted, medieval village of Lead; the Tyas and Skargill families owned the village, and the latter's timber hall (if not more buildings) were apparently still in evidence when Leland visited the area in 1558. Further on, the road joined the Ferrybridge/Tadcaster road immediately south of the village of Towton. South of the plateau, at Dinting Dale, a connecting trackway ran east to west, through the village of Saxton. The three roads thus formed a large triangle,

Reconstruction of the skull of skeleton number 16. This man, one of the oldest in the group, had blade injuries from previous engagements that had healed. One was a severe blow across the jaw with a bladed weapon, which had cut a piece of bone out from the lower jaw and also fractured it. Perhaps surprisingly, the wound had healed with no sign of infection, a tribute to medieval surgery. (Bradford University)

enclosing peaceful farmland destined to become a field of slaughter. Saxton church still stands, the churchyard now the final resting place for a number of victims of the battle. A fortified manor lay on one side of the road through the village. Ridge and furrow plough land, together with some hedgerows and woodland, have been discovered in the area of the battlefield. Leland describes how the fields of Towton and Saxton extended for some distance from the villages themselves, and notes, for example, that the land near Tadcaster was growing corn and there was some woodland. The ground north of Saxton climbed gently to form a plateau some 100ft above the surrounding ground. This plateau extended north as far as Towton, but was bisected by a gentle valley, the east end of which is known as North Acres, the western end being Towton Dale. The valley floor may have been somewhat lower in the 15th century, since centuries of agriculture may have smoothed the contours of the ground a little. To the west of the Leeds–Tadcaster road, the River Cock meandered north through meadows. The river is broader today than in the 15th century due to silting, but at the time, although narrow, it was deceptively deep. The slopes down to the river from the open ground were steep and uneven. In the snowy conditions prevailing at the time they would be slippery and treacherous, and the meadows themselves partly flooded. In a bend in the river north-west of Saxton lay Castle Hill Wood, to the north-east of which lay the open ground that was to become known as 'Bloody Meadow'. In another bend a short distance further north lay Renshaw Woods, both sets of woodland probably larger in area than they are today. To the west of the River Cock lay open fields and scattered woodland, here and there set with farms, some of which survive today. The Roman Ridge Road crossed the River Aire at Castleford, west of Pontefract, and marched northwards in a more or less straight line, passing the battlefield well to the west.

The effigy of Lord Welles, in his local church at Methley, West Yorkshire.

Dinting Dale is difficult to pinpoint, being a tract of land somewhere near Saxton, probably in the valley running east–west by the village. Andrew Boardman has suggested the ground between Saxton and Scarthingwell. However, it is just possible that it lay between Scarthingwell and Barkston Ash, where the so-called Clifford Cross once stood, and where it would have been difficult for the main Lancastrian army to see what was happening to Clifford and his men. Only Hall actually mentions Clifford as being killed at Dinting Dale, and it is possible that the surviving plinth, hollowed out for the now lost cross, has some connection, though such memorabilia are always highly suspect. Known as 'The Leper Pot', the plinth might be connected with a leper house beyond Tadcaster, but it is stretching belief a little to expect that these people would regularly travel (indeed be suffered to travel) all the way to the plinth to receive alms. Moreover, in 1835 an amateur excavation close by the turnpike road to Towton at present-day Dinting Dale unearthed human bones, which were pronounced to be those of Lord Clifford. Quite how this fact was known is a mystery, but it remains that a grave pit had been discovered in the area known today as Dinting Dale. Since it may well have been that Clifford was hurriedly buried (a family tradition says his body was 'tumbled' into a pit) there is a chance that here we have, if not perhaps the lord himself, then at least the remains of one or more of his followers.

View across Towton battlefield looking north, with the winding progression of the River Cock marked by trees on the left of the picture. The outskirts of Saxton are just visible at the bottom of the picture, with Cotcher's Lane running up from bottom centre to join the B1217. Level with this, towards the right of the picture, is a dark dot that marks the hawthorn tree. At lower extreme left, above the housing, is the loop in the river marking Castle Hill Wood, where the Lancastrians may have placed their ambush party. The area above, where the river curves towards the road, is Bloody Meadow, with Towton Dale marked by the short dark soil line that runs along to the road. The battlefield cross stands above this, at the side of the road where the light and dark fields meet. To the left are the trees of Renshaw Woods. The A162 runs up from the right to converge with the B1217 below Towton, and then runs north towards Tadcaster, visible in the far distance, towards the top of the photograph. The left-hand finger of houses in Towton village marks the line of the Old London Road, which runs left and can be traced as a thin white acute angle above the light-coloured field left of centre, as it curves towards Tadcaster. (By permission of Simmons Aerofilms Ltd)

In the village of Towton the Old London Road turned north-west to pass a manor house, Towton Hall, which appears to have been on the site since the reign of Richard II in the later 14th century. It then continued on, ascending then descending a slope to eventually meet the River Cock. There may have been a wooden bridge here, the 'Bridge of Bodies', or perhaps more probably a ford. An Italian work by Biondi notes that Lancastrians fleeing the field thought the river fordable here. From here the road eventually turned north-east to cross the River Wharfe below Tadcaster, whence it turned eastwards to York. The Wharfe would present a wider, more formidable, obstacle to a routed army than the Cock. Further south along the course of the latter as it passed the site of the battlefield there may have been another ford at Cocksford, as the name suggests, and possibly others.

The battlefield itself was thus bounded on the east by somewhat marshy ground and the west by the steep slopes leading down to the River Cock, whose waters were perhaps running quite high due to the weather. These secure flanks presumably appealed to the Lancastrian leaders and were probably one reason that Towton was picked to make a stand. The open space between was large enough to accommodate an army of the proportions that they now commanded. Beyond Towton the plateau appeared to form an ideal place to draw up the enormous divisions, sloping slightly down to the south into the dip formed by Towton Dale and North Acres.

Edward was probably desirous to get the battle over and done with, no doubt before any more enemy troops came in or the situation changed.

Lead church stands alone in the fields where the Yorkists may have had part of their camp on the night before Towton.

Pitched battles were so horribly unpredictable that it is unlikely that anyone who had any sense faced them with unshakable confidence. For the soldiery there was the prospect of death or horrific wounds, some already bearing the scars of previous encounters. For the knights and nobles, though often better armoured, there was the thought of execution at the end of the day at the hands of enemies eager to wreak vengeance on a family and its members. The two kings were playing for the highest stakes – the kingdom.

The Armies

The morning of 29 March, Palm Sunday, dawned with a leaden sky and a cutting wind. Men presumably huddled round campfires, eating as fast as they could, trying to get some hot sustenance into chilled bodies. The knights and nobles on both sides, and anyone else lucky enough, fortified themselves with wine, which gives a deceptive short-term inner warmth before actually cooling the body. Men must have been stretching and working to bring life back into cramped limbs – the Yorkists no doubt aching from the previous days' exertions. Pickets would be watching the enemy for any sign of an attack, but there was none. Doubtless priests moved through the hosts to hear confessions and to bless the armies; it was important to have God on your side in a great trial by battle. Gradually the captains began to marshal their men, retainers took position grouped around their lords, and the ponderous mass of soldiery formed up into their respective lines. If Boardman's theory is correct, then Fauconberg's vanguard was getting itself into position while the main Yorkist army was marching up the road from Sherburn-in-Elmet. Meanwhile the scouts on both sides were reporting the movements of

their enemies, as the Lancastrian forces moved through Towton village to fan out on to the plateau beyond. Waurin describes Yorkist scouts, sent ahead by the king, observing a reconnaissance party of Lancastrians and reporting back. After Edward had spoken to his cavalry, who were posted on the flank, a messenger came to warn Edward that the enemy vanguard was advancing, and the king went to take position behind his banners.

Exactly where these two great armies stood is not known for certain, but since the battlefield is relatively undisturbed and the features remain largely unchanged, likely positions can be surmised. The two ridges of the plateau, cut by the valley, offered areas of obvious advantage, that to the north being the most likely area for the Lancastrian army to occupy. The eastern flank was afforded some protection by sloping ground down to the road, with trees and marsh beyond, the western flank by the steep, slippery slopes leading to the River Cock. In front the ground sloped gradually into the depression before rising to the second, southern, ridge. Moreover the width, at some 1,000 yards, afforded a generous space in which to marshal the type of army fielded by the Lancastrians. To the south, the second plateau, reflecting the angle of the road, was 500 yards wider.

An alternative formation has been suggested, in which the Lancastrian army was drawn up with its eastern flank near the vantage point of the hawthorn tree, which, with the triangulation point north of North Acres, is not only 150ft high but has steeper slopes than much of the eastern side. Thus it is possible that from here the Lancastrian line ran on a south-west axis, to the Saxton road that meets the B1217.

The slopes leading down to the River Cock, from Renshaw Woods, looking south.

The slopes from Renshaw
Woods to the Cock, looking
north-westwards.

However, this would have placed the slopes and River Cock at the back of the army, which would severely hamper any chance of retreat, should things go wrong. This would also have necessitated their enemies attacking up the southern slopes of the southern plateau from the start, which would have created such a disadvantage (remembering also that Norfolk's division had seemingly still not arrived) that it must surely have resulted in a Yorkist defeat.

Thus we may assume that the Lancastrians initially drew up their divisions in a line across the northern ridge. The Yorkists, meanwhile, camped in the vicinity of Lead, Dinting Dale and Saxton, and with the main body perhaps marching directly from Sherburn-in-Elmet, assembled on the southern ridge north of Saxton village, and began their advance.

The Lancastrians are supposed to have secretly sent a force of cavalry down to Castle Hill Wood, in which they now waited for an opportunity to ambush their enemies. Only Waurin reports this ruse, though there is no reason to suppose it could not have occurred. Somerset was in command, and it is possible that he had witnessed the use of ambush at the battle of Wakefield the previous year.

The Lancastrians were at least fresh. Edward must have been aware of his army's lack of numbers, and inwardly anxious as to the whereabouts of Norfolk. He knew his men were tired, but they were tough and, moreover, had the moral advantage of having routed the Lancastrians at Ferrybridge the previous day. So on that bitter morning perhaps some 25,000 Lancastrians waited to confront 20,000 Yorkists. Hall asserts that at first the Lancastrians ranged across the northern ridge could not see their enemies, coming up from the direction of Saxton in battle order. This was because the Yorkist forces, whether along the line of Saxton and Lead, or marching up the Ferrybridge/Towton road, or both, were out of sight on the rear slopes of the southern ridge. As the first troops crested the top of the ridge they saw the enemy on the northern ridge and a great shout went up. At the same time, says Hall, it started to snow. The weather conditions are attested by *Hearne's Fragment* and by the *Croyland Chronicle*, **49**

Looking north towards Castle Hill Wood, from where the Lancastrian surprise attack is said to have come. In the foreground stands one of the small mounds whose date has yet to be confirmed.

both of which are vague enough to be interpreted as meaning that it snowed throughout the battle or in intermittent showers. 'No quarter' was the word passed around both armies. The day would be bitter in every meaning of the word.

To the watching Lancastrians it must have seemed in the grey light that the earth was suddenly belching forth men, as a long dark line slowly sprouted seemingly out of the ground. It ran from the road on one side to the slopes of the river on the other, and as it moved, more and more ranks appeared. There is no record of exactly how the Yorkist divisions were formed, but if flanking movements were to be avoided then both armies can only have been set out in line, rather than column. The traditional medieval army was split into three divisions, the vanward (or vaward), mainward and rearward. We simply do not know whether this was employed here, nor whether the divisions were set out side by side, or one behind the other. It seems most plausible that the three divisions were set out one behind the other, and that the right flank of the Yorkist army was probably set about the hawthorn tree on the east of the field, giving the added height and security of steep slopes. For the most part we do not know where the commanders stood, or who commanded which division. Edward had raised the Black Bull of Clarence, his family standard borne by Ralph Vestynden, and logic demands that he must have commanded the main division. Warwick was presumably there too, but it is not known how his forces were disposed either. Edward may have commanded the mainward as a central division, with Warwick bringing up the rearward behind. Given Warwick's poor record in battle as a tactician, his defensive predilection, and the fact that he was nursing a wounded leg, he may have been formed in rear. Perhaps instead their divisions were set side by side, Edward on the left and Warwick on the right. The pressure applied by the Yorkist right against the Lancastrians opposite seems to have been more successful than the Yorkist left, suggesting perhaps that this was the work of a strong central division rather than one commanded by Warwick. Lord Fauconberg appears to have led out the troops of the van to form a line in front of the main host. Again the position of the van is not certain; some have placed Fauconberg on the right of the main line, but this does not logically follow through the chronicler's descriptions of the archery duel, since only a portion of the enemy line would then be involved. It is quite plausible to imagine that, rather than compose the vanguard of archers, billmen and men-at-arms, Fauconberg instead led out a mass of archers, perhaps some 10,000 men in this long formation, designed to line up against the enemy. The rearguard, under Sir John Wenlock, Sir John Dinham and others, would have included 'prickers', light horsemen who not only checked deserters with their lances, but were useful in the rout to ride down fleeing enemy soldiers. Behind, probably somewhere in the vicinity of the villages of Lead and perhaps Saxton, stood the great baggage park, where sat chaplains, pages, baggage boys and, possibly, some washer-women. Here were tethered a great mass of horses, palfreys for transport to the field, warhorses fully accoutred for instant action, though most of the knights were to fight on foot in the manner now most usual in battle. Here too were posted sumpter horses or mules, to supplement the waggons.

On the other side of the small valley the mass of the Lancastrian army stood. The front was also composed of archers. The Duke of Somerset commanded the army but again we are not certain where he was positioned. The Earl of Northumberland appears to have been positioned on the left (eastern) flank of the Lancastrian mainward, though some reconstructions have placed him on the right. Many other lords no doubt packed the main division; Hall notes that Sir Andrew Trollope and Northumberland were 'chieftains' in the vanguard. The rear was commanded by the Duke of Exeter and Lord Wilton. The Lancastrian army was huge, a mass of bristling weapons stretching from the road, with

The cross at the side of the B1217, decked with flowers in remembrance of those who perished in the battle. In the distance lies Bloody Meadow. Probably of 15th-century date, the cross may have been made to commemorate the battle, been set up earlier simply as a wayside cross, formed part of Clifford's monument with the 'Leper Pot' cross foundation, or possibly comes from Richard III's chapel. The head is shown in one 19th-century engraving lying in bushes by the wayside, referred to as 'Lord Dacre's Cross', but there is no firm connection. It was restored in 1929, and the inscription is modern.

View from the cross looking south towards Bloody Meadow.

its marshy flank on the east, to the slopes of the River Cock to the west. Somewhere in the host near to the Duke of Somerset fluttered the royal banner, reminding the men that King Henry was there in spirit if not in body.

There is a possibility that the Yorkists actually arrived on the field first. Vergil mentions that King Henry gave a speech to the troops (though in reality he was not present, so he probably mistakes him for Somerset) but, when it was finished, was forced to sound the alarm that the enemy was advancing. It would give some reason to the rather cramped position the Lancastrians adopted on the northern ridge. However, this position may well have been deliberate. On the western side there was no reason for Edward to extend his line to the edge of the slopes down to the River Cock. As his men advanced they would then have to cluster together as the river bent inwards and the frontage narrowed, and if they were attacked, the men on the far left of the Yorkist line would not be able to fight or shoot at their enemies, who would be advancing to their right. If, in contrast, the Lancastrians stood their ground, they occupied a position that offered no alternative to a frontal assault uphill. This, however, rather depended on how well they faired against the enemy archers.

Hall says the armies formed up at 9.00am. Between them lay the valley formed by North Acres on the east and Towton Dale on the west. Both sides were ranged along their respective heights, freezing in the cold wind. The wind, however, was now blowing from the south into the faces of the Lancastrians, and whipping the snow along with it. No doubt Somerset was happy to let the smaller Yorkist force climb the slopes and, unable to outflank his superior and rested army, to dash itself to pieces against it. Edward must have occasionally looked back and wondered when and if the Duke of Norfolk was going to arrive to strengthen his own lines, and possibly bring artillery.

FAUCONBERG'S ADVANCE

Seasoned campaigners knew how to use the weather, and it was Lord Fauconberg, victor of the previous day's chase, who would employ it to his advantage. When all was ready, he gave the order for the archers to advance. A wall of men began moving forward, plodding down the forward slope of their own hill towards the vast host confronting them. They came on slowly so as not to lose formation, feet frozen and fingers probably numb. It was Fauconberg's task to use his archers to create the artillery barrage with which the battle was to begin. The men may well have been arranged in chequerboard formation (the 'herse' or 'harrow' arrangement mentioned at Agincourt) with each rank staggered between those before and behind for maximum vision and room to manoeuvre. The archers knew exactly when they had reached effective range, probably some 200–300 yards from the enemy. Here they halted, but Fauconberg had not planned on a simple archery duel. The decimation inflicted by English archers in the French wars had been so effective because the enemy made little use of longbows, instead relying on the slower crossbow. In this English civil war, however, the fearful longbowmen confronted each other, tending to cancel each other out.

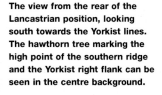

The view from the rear of the Lancastrian position, looking south towards the Yorkist lines. The hawthorn tree marking the high point of the southern ridge and the Yorkist right flank can be seen in the centre background.

Now Fauconberg would use the wind and snow to good effect. Edward Hall is the only chronicler to describe the next move, which he does in detail.

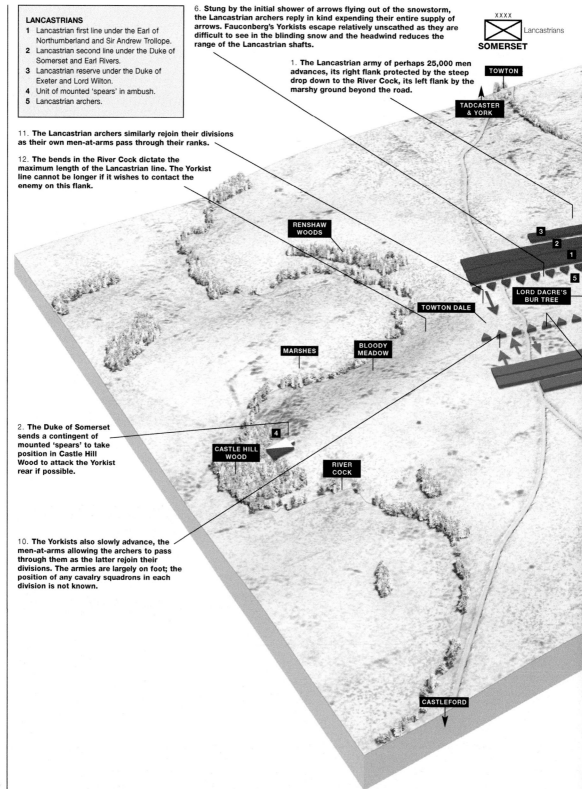

LANCASTRIANS

1 Lancastrian first line under the Earl of Northumberland and Sir Andrew Trollope.
2 Lancastrian second line under the Duke of Somerset and Earl Rivers.
3 Lancastrian reserve under the Duke of Exeter and Lord Wilton.
4 Unit of mounted 'spears' in ambush.
5 Lancastrian archers.

6. Stung by the initial shower of arrows flying out of the snowstorm, the Lancastrian archers reply in kind expending their entire supply of arrows. Fauconberg's Yorkists escape relatively unscathed as they are difficult to see in the blinding snow and the headwind reduces the range of the Lancastrian shafts.

XXXX
Lancastrians
SOMERSET

1. The Lancastrian army of perhaps 25,000 men advances, its right flank protected by the steep drop down to the River Cock, its left flank by the marshy ground beyond the road.

TOWTON

TADCASTER & YORK

11. The Lancastrian archers similarly rejoin their divisions as their own men-at-arms pass through their ranks.

12. The bends in the River Cock dictate the maximum length of the Lancastrian line. The Yorkist line cannot be longer if it wishes to contact the enemy on this flank.

3
2
1
5

RENSHAW WOODS

LORD DACRE'S BUR TREE

TOWTON DALE

MARSHES

BLOODY MEADOW

2. The Duke of Somerset sends a contingent of mounted 'spears' to take position in Castle Hill Wood to attack the Yorkist rear if possible.

4

CASTLE HILL WOOD

RIVER COCK

10. The Yorkists also slowly advance, the men-at-arms allowing the archers to pass through them as the latter rejoin their divisions. The armies are largely on foot; the position of any cavalry squadrons in each division is not known.

CASTLEFORD

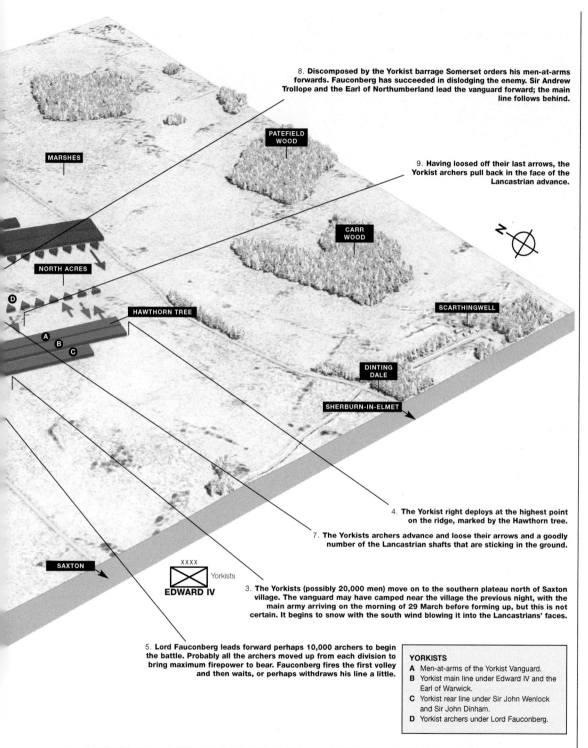

8. Discomposed by the Yorkist barrage Somerset orders his men-at-arms forwards. Fauconberg has succeeded in dislodging the enemy. Sir Andrew Trollope and the Earl of Northumberland lead the vanguard forward; the main line follows behind.

9. Having loosed off their last arrows, the Yorkist archers pull back in the face of the Lancastrian advance.

MARSHES

PATEFIELD WOOD

CARR WOOD

NORTH ACRES

SCARTHINGWELL

HAWTHORN TREE

A
B
C

DINTING DALE

SHERBURN-IN-ELMET

4. The Yorkist right deploys at the highest point on the ridge, marked by the Hawthorn tree.

7. The Yorkists archers advance and loose their arrows and a goodly number of the Lancastrian shafts that are sticking in the ground.

SAXTON

XXXX
Yorkists
EDWARD IV

3. The Yorkists (possibly 20,000 men) move on to the southern plateau north of Saxton village. The vanguard may have camped near the village the previous night, with the main army arriving on the morning of 29 March before forming up, but this is not certain. It begins to snow with the south wind blowing it into the Lancastrians' faces.

5. Lord Fauconberg leads forward perhaps 10,000 archers to begin the battle. Probably all the archers moved up from each division to bring maximum firepower to bear. Fauconberg fires the first volley and then waits, or perhaps withdraws his line a little.

YORKISTS	
A	Men-at-arms of the Yorkist Vanguard.
B	Yorkist main line under Edward IV and the Earl of Warwick.
C	Yorkist rear line under Sir John Wenlock and Sir John Dinham.
D	Yorkist archers under Lord Fauconberg.

BATTLE OF TOWTON – THE ARCHERY DUEL

29 March 1461, viewed from the south-west showing the initial advance of both Yorkist and Lancastrian armies and the attack of Fauconberg's Yorkist archers.

Edward IV in full armour, as depicted in the late 15th-century *Rous Roll*. (By permission of the British Library, Add. 48976, Figure 16)

The lord Fauconberg, which led the foreward of Edward's battle being a man of great policy and of much experience of martial feats caused every archer under his standard to shoot one flight and then made them stand still. The northern men, feeling the shoot, but by reason of the snow, not perfectly viewing the distance between them and their enemies [the snow and wind was driving into the Lancastrian faces from the south] *like hardy men shot their sheaf arrows as fast as they might, but all their shot was lost and their labour in vain for they came not near the southern men by forty tailors yards.*

So precise is Hall's description that it smacks of a story passed down of a novel battle situation. Fauconberg's archers were ordered to loose one volley and then to pause. The ruse worked. As he suspected, the Lancastrian archers were having trouble in the blinding snow and, for the most part, probably did not even see the deadly shafts until they came flying out of the snow and struck them down. The response was immediate. All along the line bowmen knocked their arrows and began to shoot, perhaps not even clearly seeing the enemy at whom they were shooting. As Fauconberg predicted, the effects of the weather told on the Lancastrian response. The wind coming straight at them had the effect of depressing the arrows so that they fell short. Hall's estimate of a shortfall of 40 tailor's yards seems quite high, considering that archers would be experienced at their trade, and would be expected to compensate for even a strong head wind. He may have exaggerated, or else the snow was blinding and made the enemy difficult to see. Either way, the Lancastrians continued to shoot until they had exhausted their supplies of arrows – usually a sheaf of 24, though extra sheafs may have been brought up before the battle commenced. The ground in front of Fauconberg's men was a mass of wooden shafts. His men now marched forward again, and began to send their own arrows into the enemy ranks. As well as these, they retrieved enemy arrows and sent them back too, though Fauconberg ordered that they leave half the arrows in the ground to impede the enemy when they advanced. As Hall puts it: *When their shot was almost spent the Lord Fauconberg marched forward with his archers, who not only shot their own sheaves, but also gathered the arrows of their enemies and let a great part fly against their own masters, and another part they let stand on the ground which sore annoyed the legs of the owners when battle was joined.*

The Lancastrians now suffered further as arrows came whistling out of the murk into their ranks in a continuous stream. Boardman commented that this may have been the biggest archery battle in English history. If 10,000 Yorkist archers were involved, shooting up to 12 arrows per minute, then some 120,000 shafts could have been in the air in any one minute, and at least some 30,000 at any one moment. Most of the heads would be of the dual-purpose or bodkin varieties, capable of punching through mail and in some cases of boring through plate armour. Men in the Lancastrian line must have felt horribly vulnerable. The knights and other men-at-arms in plate armour did not carry a shield, while the less well-armed billmen and bowmen had at best a small buckler that was not designed for deflecting missiles. The legs of archers and billmen would be largely unprotected, and flesh was no obstacle. Arrows whirred and buzzed past like angry insects, or struck armour plate like the clatter of hailstones, and here and there men crumpled or fell screaming.

Looking north towards the
Lancastrian line from the
hawthorn tree. (Photograph by
Graham Turner)

THE LANCASTRIAN ATTACK

At some point the order was given for the Lancastrian host to advance. Men lay dead or wounded all along their front, others being pulled to the rear with shafts sprouting from all parts of the body. Somerset had decided his troops could not just stand there and die without retaliating; that was guaranteed to undermine their morale. Fauconberg had achieved his objective. He had managed to sting the enemy into moving from his defended position. Now, as he watched the dim mass of men moving forward, he knew he must retire to allow the men-at-arms to take over. His archers drew back as the Lancastrians advanced through their own ranks of bowmen.

Jean de Waurin recounts that Edward rode along the ranks 'where all the nobles were' and reminded them how they had all wanted to make him king and how his rights had been usurped. He repeated that if any man did not wish to fight, he should leave. *So all of them hearing this good request by the young king, shouted in unison that they would follow him until death if need be. Hearing this good support, the king thanked them and he jumped down from his horse and told them, sword in hand, that he would live or die with them in order to give them courage.*

Waurin asserts that Somerset and Earl Rivers were the first to launch the attack. Shouting 'King Henry! King Henry!' ranks of men-at-arms marched noisily together down the slope, those bannerets having a square or oblong banner with their coat-of-arms proudly displayed. About them were their retainers, mainly wearing plate armour or part plate and brigandine. Here and there fluttered the long standards that

57

The Opening Barrage.
Fauconberg's Yorkist archers
loose off their last arrows as the
men-at-arms advance through
them to meet the oncoming
Lancastrians. The experienced
Fauconberg had goaded the
Lancastrian archers, blinded by
the snow blowing into their
faces, into squandering their
arrows in ineffective volleys. His
Yorkist archers then advanced
and poured perhaps upwards of
300,000 shafts into the
Lancastrian ranks, returning
many of the Lancastrian arrows
against their owners for good
measure. Unwilling to suffer this
deadly bombardment
impassively, the Lancastrians
advanced off their ridge towards
the Yorkist lines opposite.
(courtesy of the artist, Graham
Turner)

served as rallying points for the men of a lord. Together they came on in a solid wall, until they reached the arrows deliberately left sticking in the ground by the Yorkist archers. They thrust through them and on across the valley floor to the slope of the southern plateau. Ahead the Yorkist men-at-arms were now moving to greet them, as the archers slipped through the ranks to let the richer members of society do what they were trained from youth to do. It was probably still difficult for the Lancastrians to see their opponents properly, as the snow still obscured the view. But they were rested and confident in their numbers, and eager to take retribution for the arrows.

The two bodies probably met somewhere on the forward slope of the southern ridge. The Lancastrian left under Northumberland may have been slower in moving forward than the rest, which may have resulted in a slight change in the axis of the lines, as the western end pushed further forward. With a great shout and clash of weapons the two sides collided. Now came the bloody business of hand-to-hand combat. The retainers knew they must look out for their lord and to that effect no-one would be too keen to push forward too far without support, apart from which such a move would be suicidal in the press. Their effectiveness lay in keeping tight and preventing any ingress by the enemy. Much of this combat must have been a thrusting match with the sharp ends of staff weapons. Here and their a chance was taken to deliver a swinging blow with axe-head, hammer or beak. Even knights and others who bore swords at their belts would often carry a pollaxe or halberd as their main weapon. It not only provided several varieties of blow but gave more reach than was possible with an arming sword. The hook or beak on a halberd or pollaxe could trip the unwary. But all this was tiring work. Men were trained to fight hard and endure strain; their armour was not felt to be a great encumbrance. But it

was hot to wear and even fit men will begin to feel fatigue after constant combat with weapons. Then one slip was enough to let through an enemy point. As well as the problem of tiredness, the number of dead and wounded began slowly to mount. Both sides fought stubbornly to hold their ground, and those in authority must have tried to refresh the lines by sending through troops from the rear ranks. Some of those who fell wounded were finished off by excited opponents, others were trampled in the chaos, while still others were dragged back out of the press by companions.

The push by the Yorkist right against Northumberland may have swung the line even further askew, and it may have been around this time that the earl himself was severely wounded and dragged from the fight, an occurrence that always threatened panic in a medieval army. On the Yorkist left, however, there was no such progress. On the contrary, the superior numbers of Lancastrians was beginning to tell, as Edward's soldiers were slowly pushed back across the top of the plateau. It was probably at this time that the Lancastrians used their secret weapon.

View of the Lancastrian line, looking north towards Towton.

The Surprise Attack
It is said that a group of Lancastrian 'spears' (a term denoting either infantry or cavalry, but here almost certainly horsemen with lances) was positioned in Castle Hill Wood before the battle, ready to deliver a surprise attack on the Yorkist left. Only Waurin mentions this episode, however, which tends to cast some doubt on its validity. Yet if one looks at

the initial positions the two armies are thought to have occupied, then the idea behind the move gains credibility. It is quite likely, as has been said, that initially the Lancastrians had no great interest in moving from their position on the northern of the two ridges. Secure in their flanks and with an uphill attack the only alternative, they presented a similar problem for the Yorkists as had faced Duke William at Hastings. It was only the decisive use of the archers by Fauconberg that seems to have impelled them to make the first move and come down towards the Yorkists. Had Fauconberg not used this tactic or not used it successfully, then the main Yorkist force would have probably advanced instead. The meandering course of the River Cock meant that the left flank of the Yorkists would only be protected at some points on the field, where the river bends inwards. Had they marched forwards and engaged, their left flank and rear would have been exposed to a charge of mounted men-at-arms from the woods. This could have had a devastating effect on Edward's left wing, which may have rapidly spread along the ranks. Panic can prove infectious, especially amongst tired men facing great odds.

As things turned out, the advance by the Lancastrians meant the Yorkists did not have to move nearly as far forward to meet them. Moreover, though the Yorkists were still open to a flank attack, the route now forced on the horsemen was over rougher ground. The attack would not strike home to such effect. Nevertheless, there is evidence to suggest that, by this stage, the battle was not going too well for the Yorkists. Hall, despite writing for a Tudor court, praised Edward's

Bloody Meadow. This area twice saw fierce fighting, once when the Yorkist left almost gave way and again when the Lancastrian line crumbled. (Photograph by Graham Turner)

View looking south-east, from Renshaw Woods past the extreme westerly end of the Lancastrian line (far left) towards the Yorkists, their right marked by the hawthorn tree and their left by the clump of bushes. To the right of the B1217 road is Bloody Meadow.

fighting qualities, how he: 'so courageously comforted his men, refreshing the weary, and helping the wounded.'

It is possible, of course, that this simply refers to sections in which the ebb and flow of battle was starting to take its toll, but it would fit quite well to a surprise attack by the 200 'spears', who suddenly appeared and came crashing into the left of the Yorkist line. If this scenario is correct, then the natural result would be for the Yorkists to fall back on their left flank, as men tried to escape or press together for safety and to prevent the horsemen from penetrating further into their ranks. Since the right wing may well have been more successful and pressed back the slow-moving division under the Earl of Northumberland, the fighting line of the two armies may well have pivoted at least 45 degrees from where it had started, and perhaps even more.

Despite the apparent success of his right wing in holding and pushing back the Lancastrians opposed to it, the pressure on the rest of Edward's army was starting to tell. The more rested and larger enemy formation was able to channel larger numbers of fresh troops into the front ranks. The fighting was now on top of the southern ridge, as the Yorkists were slowly but surely pushed back towards the southern slopes leading to Saxton village. A field of dead and wounded marked the passage of the fighting behind the Lancastrians, from the slopes around North Acres to the aptly named Bloody Meadow. The crisis of the battle had been reached. If Somerset could push the Yorkists over the edge on to the downward southern slopes, the line would break and men would turn and run helter-skelter back through Saxton. It just needed a little more hard fighting and relentless pressure to tip the balance and secure a Lancastrian victory.

THE MELEE AT TOWTON (pages 62–63)

The snow at Towton made the struggle doubly bitter. After the initial barrage of arrows, the main battle developed between the long lines of men-at-arms, a mixture of richer individuals in full plate armour and others in varying amounts of less expensive equipment. Men stood close alongside their fellow retainers, both for protection and moral support, as comrades fought under the eyes of their friends. In the front ranks of the Lancastrian line, retainers of the Earl of Devon, distinguished by their white boar badges (1), strive to push back the Yorkists opposing them. A Lancastrian is clad in armour of west European style (2); the points (ties) securing his *pauldron* to the shoulder and *couter* to the elbow can be clearly seen. By contrast, the plate armour worn by the figure on the extreme left (3) has a *couter* attached to the upper and lower cannons (arm pieces) by internal leather strips, the rivets of which can be seen. The leather straps that fasten the two halves of the cuirass and *fauld* (skirt of hoops) can be seen down the side below the armpit. On the wearer's left side the armour is held by hinges with removable pins; being of metal it made them less easy to cut on this more vulnerable side. A retainer wearing a brigandine and *sallet* lies face down; the clusters of rivet heads on the brigandine mark the small plates that line this form of armour (4). A man in a quilted jack is sprawled across him (5). Jacks were cheaper to produce, usually being made from numerous layers of linen to produce a surprisingly effective defence. Behind the Yorkist frontline fly standards of Edward IV bearing the white rose en soleil (6). One retainer wearing this badge has a sword and buckler by his side but prefers to use a glaive as his first weapon (7). Staff weapons allowed enemy soldiers to more easily be held at arm's reach, and combat may have consisted largely of the two lines thrusting at each other to find gaps, or trying to hook opponents off balance. A forest of staff weapons rises behind, many being English bills (8). Fighting fiercely, William Herbert bears his coat-of-arms of three lions on his heraldic tabard (9). He uses a sword of diamond section with its rigid blade to thrust at the gap under the sallet of his opponent. In this picture we have chosen to portray him in a north Italian armour with its typical style of helmet, an *armet*. Here the lower face is additionally protected by a wrapper, fastened by a strap at the rear. As can be seen, however, *sallets* are by far the most popular form of head protection in England, though a soldier at far right wears a kettle hat with a wide brim all round (10). To the right, Walter Devereux wears a white tabard (11); both he and Herbert would later be created lords. On the far right flies the standard of Edmund, Lord Grey of Ruthin, with its black ragged staffs (12).
(Graham Turner)

The view from the northern ridge looking towards Towton, ground over which the broken Lancastrians would have fled. The slopes down to the River Cock are beyond the left-hand edge of the picture. The road is the B1217.

THE TIDE TURNS

It may have been the desperate situation on the Yorkist left, as it was pushed ever nearer to the slopes, and perhaps also harried by the surprise attack from the woods, that caused Edward to thrust himself into the weakest spots on the left of the line. A giant clad in armour, with the Black Bull of Clarence fluttering above him, he inspired confidence wherever he went. A king was demonstrating just why he was a privileged member of the ruling class. Where the battle was thickest, he was there leading from the front, fighting to keep men's spirits up and bolster morale. It must have helped enormously to be so close to the person for whom so many were willing to lay down their lives, and to see him risking his with them. However popular King Henry was, his symbolic presence represented by a flag could not hope to have the same effect.

At some juncture the division of the Duke of Norfolk at last appeared on the road from Ferrybridge. It is not known for certain if John Mowbray had come with his men, or whether he was too ill to join them in this final act and had stayed behind, perhaps at Pontefract. Equally, it is not known if any artillery had come with him and, if it had, whether this was dragged on to the field. There is no reference to the use of it in any of the chronicles, nor have any cannonballs or other items relating to cannon been discovered on the site itself. It may be that, worried that his men might arrive too late, the Duke decided to leave the artillery at Pontefract, especially if the bridge at Ferrybridge was only a temporary structure of beams and planks. Only *Hearne's Fragment* mentions the arrival of Norfolk by name and, given his comment on the timing of the

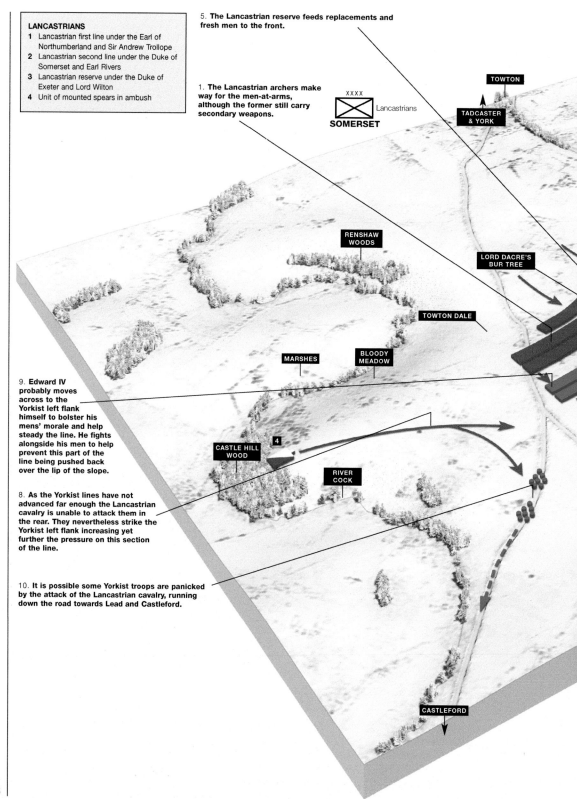

LANCASTRIANS
1. Lancastrian first line under the Earl of Northumberland and Sir Andrew Trollope
2. Lancastrian second line under the Duke of Somerset and Earl Rivers
3. Lancastrian reserve under the Duke of Exeter and Lord Wilton
4. Unit of mounted spears in ambush

5. **The Lancastrian reserve feeds replacements and fresh men to the front.**

1. **The Lancastrian archers make way for the men-at-arms, although the former still carry secondary weapons.**

xxxx
SOMERSET Lancastrians

TOWTON

TADCASTER & YORK

RENSHAW WOODS

LORD DACRE'S BUR TREE

TOWTON DALE

MARSHES

BLOODY MEADOW

9. **Edward IV probably moves across to the Yorkist left flank himself to bolster his mens' morale and help steady the line. He fights alongside his men to help prevent this part of the line being pushed back over the lip of the slope.**

CASTLE HILL WOOD

4

RIVER COCK

8. **As the Yorkist lines have not advanced far enough the Lancastrian cavalry is unable to attack them in the rear. They nevertheless strike the Yorkist left flank increasing yet further the pressure on this section of the line.**

10. **It is possible some Yorkist troops are panicked by the attack of the Lancastrian cavalry, running down the road towards Lead and Castleford.**

CASTLEFORD

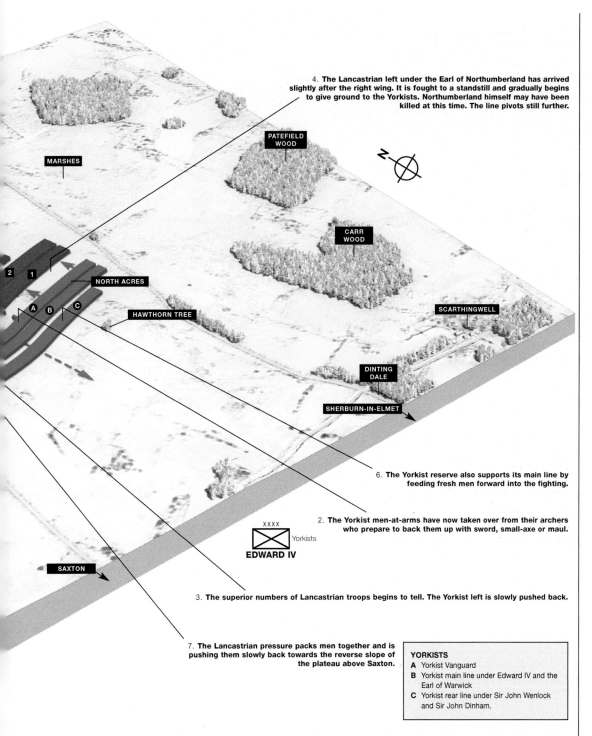

4. The Lancastrian left under the Earl of Northumberland has arrived slightly after the right wing. It is fought to a standstill and gradually begins to give ground to the Yorkists. Northumberland himself may have been killed at this time. The line pivots still further.

PATEFIELD WOOD

MARSHES

N

CARR WOOD

2 1

NORTH ACRES

A B C

SCARTHINGWELL

HAWTHORN TREE

DINTING DALE

SHERBURN-IN-ELMET

6. The Yorkist reserve also supports its main line by feeding fresh men forward into the fighting.

xxxx
Yorkists
EDWARD IV

2. The Yorkist men-at-arms have now taken over from their archers who prepare to back them up with sword, small-axe or maul.

3. The superior numbers of Lancastrian troops begins to tell. The Yorkist left is slowly pushed back.

SAXTON

7. The Lancastrian pressure packs men together and is pushing them slowly back towards the reverse slope of the plateau above Saxton.

> **YORKISTS**
> **A** Yorkist Vanguard
> **B** Yorkist main line under Edward IV and the Earl of Warwick
> **C** Yorkist rear line under Sir John Wenlock and Sir John Dinham.

BATTLE OF TOWTON – THE LANCASTRIAN PUSH

29 March 1461, viewed from the south-west showing the fierce melee as the Yorkist and Lancastrian lines slowly pivot. The Lancastrian numbers begin to tell and the Yorkists are in danger of being driven down the slope of the hill.

battle all through the night, he must be treated with caution. … *when about the noon the foresaid John Duke of Norfolk with a fresh band of good men of war came in, to the aid of the new elected King Edward.* However, Vergil also notes that: *Thus did the fight continue for more than 10 hours in equal balance, when at last King Henry* [in fact the Duke of Somerset] *espied the forces of his foe increase, and his own somewhat yield* … Moreover, George Neville in his letter to Coppini remarks on the bravery in the battle of King Edward, the Duke of Norfolk and Neville's own brother and uncle.

The reference by Vergil to a ten-hour battle seems excessive, but there is no doubt it was hard fought and neither side wanted to give way when such important issues were at stake. The duration of this battle was certainly far longer than usual, and those involved must have been exhausted. The sight of fresh troops would have been soul destroying. At first it was probably not obvious to those engaged in hard combat that more soldiers were arriving. The new men, presumably both mounted

Prince Arthur's Book of 1519, showing at top the swan badge of Henry VI with his livery colours of blue and white, with below his royal arms impaling those of his wife, Margaret of Anjou. Below is the white lion of March (for Mortimer), a badge of Edward IV, with his livery colours of blue and red, the white rose *en soleil* and suns in splendour. Below are his arms impaling those of his wife, Elizabeth Woodville. (College of Arms, Ms Vincent 152, p.53)

Standards illustrated in an early 16th-century manuscript. The red cross of St George is represented at the fly. The upper example appears to show the heraldic antelope of the House of Lancaster. The Yorkist livery colours fill the main area of the lower flag, with badges of the white lion of March and white roses. (College of Arms, Ms M1.2, p.5)

and on foot, began to appear on the right of the Yorkist line and increasingly to thicken and extend it. They may even have swung in on the exposed left wing of the Lancastrian army. The pressure was now against the latter. It may have been at this point, as Somerset's men realised that large numbers of fresh troops were arriving, that those in rear began to slip away. Weighing up the situation, they did not like what they saw. The Duke of Somerset himself and other nobles who escaped the carnage must have called for their horses as soon as they realised the battle was swinging the other way, otherwise they would have been lucky to escape the press. Vergil suggests that Somerset (here confused with Henry VI) tried to encourage his men as the new Yorkist division flooded on to the field, but that he also moved a little way from the press prudently to watch the course of events: ...*he with a few horsemen removing a little out of that place, expected the event of the fight, but behold, suddenly his soldiers gave back, which when he saw this he fled also.*

Once the banners of the commanders were seen to leave, it would not take much for their followers to pull out and follow. As soon as it became obvious that it was every man for himself, the Lancastrian line would start to collapse. Once a trickle had begun, it did not take long for it to become a flood. Heartened, the rest of Edward's army fought on, and at last the Lancastrian line crumbled.

THE ROUT

Those who left earliest from the rear probably had the best chance of escape. Many Lancastrian soldiers were still engaged in the fighting and it was very dangerous to fall back and turn to run when in the front ranks faced by an enemy. There were now real problems caused by the lay of the land. The secure flank favoured by Somerset when taking up position, with the River Cock on the flank, was now to become a death-trap.

As men began to break and run, many soon found that their options for escape were severely limited. Those who ran to the western slopes

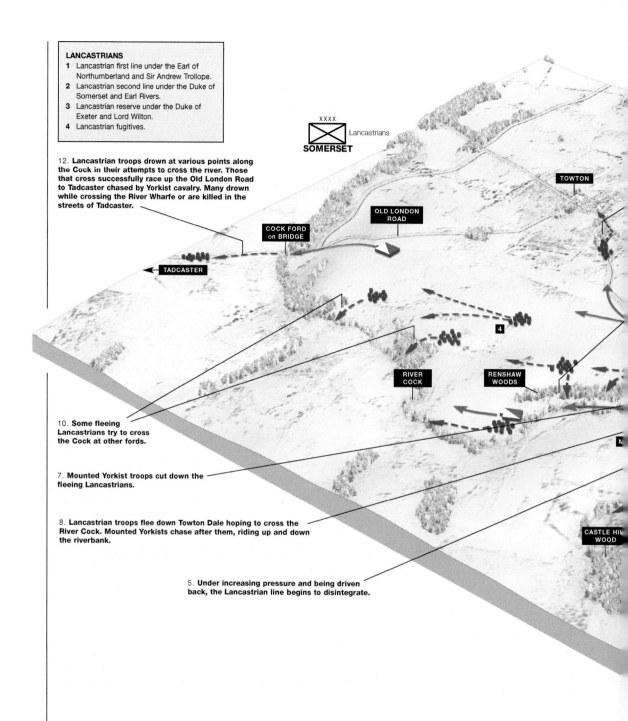

LANCASTRIANS
1 Lancastrian first line under the Earl of Northumberland and Sir Andrew Trollope.
2 Lancastrian second line under the Duke of Somerset and Earl Rivers.
3 Lancastrian reserve under the Duke of Exeter and Lord Wilton.
4 Lancastrian fugitives.

12. Lancastrian troops drown at various points along the Cock in their attempts to cross the river. Those that cross successfully race up the Old London Road to Tadcaster chased by Yorkist cavalry. Many drown while crossing the River Wharfe or are killed in the streets of Tadcaster.

XXXX
Lancastrians
SOMERSET

TOWTON

OLD LONDON ROAD

COCK FORD OR BRIDGE

TADCASTER

4

RIVER COCK

RENSHAW WOODS

10. Some fleeing Lancastrians try to cross the Cock at other fords.

7. Mounted Yorkist troops cut down the fleeing Lancastrians.

8. Lancastrian troops flee down Towton Dale hoping to cross the River Cock. Mounted Yorkists chase after them, riding up and down the riverbank.

CASTLE HILL WOOD

5. Under increasing pressure and being driven back, the Lancastrian line begins to disintegrate.

BATTLE OF TOWTON – THE ROUT

29 March 1461, viewed from the west-south-west showing the arrival of the Duke of Norfolk's division and the resurgence of the Yorkist line. The Lancastrians break in rout and the Yorkists begin a bloody pursuit.

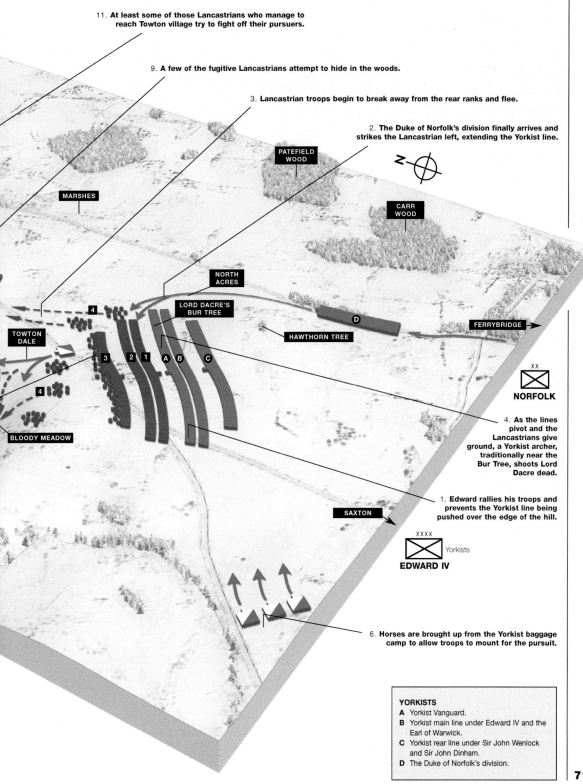

11. At least some of those Lancastrians who manage to reach Towton village try to fight off their pursuers.

9. A few of the fugitive Lancastrians attempt to hide in the woods.

3. Lancastrian troops begin to break away from the rear ranks and flee.

2. The Duke of Norfolk's division finally arrives and strikes the Lancastrian left, extending the Yorkist line.

PATEFIELD WOOD

N

MARSHES

CARR WOOD

NORTH ACRES

LORD DACRE'S BUR TREE

4

D

FERRYBRIDGE

HAWTHORN TREE

TOWTON DALE

3   2   1   A   B   C

XX

NORFOLK

4

4. As the lines pivot and the Lancastrians give ground, a Yorkist archer, traditionally near the Bur Tree, shoots Lord Dacre dead.

BLOODY MEADOW

1. Edward rallies his troops and prevents the Yorkist line being pushed over the edge of the hill.

SAXTON

XXXX

Yorkists

EDWARD IV

6. Horses are brought up from the Yorkist baggage camp to allow troops to mount for the pursuit.

YORKISTS
A Yorkist Vanguard.
B Yorkist main line under Edward IV and the Earl of Warwick.
C Yorkist rear line under Sir John Wenlock and Sir John Dinham.
D The Duke of Norfolk's division.

71

View of the valley between the ridges, down which Lancastrian fugitives would have fled, attempting to reach the River Cock. (Thom Richardson)

leading down to the river and went headlong over the edge would realise that the gradient was steep and slippery from the wet and snow. It sent some of them sliding down to the river bank. Behind the army lay Bloody Meadow; as the Lancastrian lines broke up and began to run, they were cut down as they fled across Bloody Meadow in an attempt to get clear of the fighting and the plateau. Others found, north of Bloody Meadow, that the gentler slopes between the two ridges forming the valley known as Towton Dale created a sort of funnel that led westward to the river. It was the only access route that did not involve harsh gradients, and many no doubt ran along the Dale in the hope of reaching the River Cock and safety. However, it is fairly safe to assume that the Yorkists also saw this route. Many of Norfolk's division were no doubt already mounted, while many other men-at-arms, especially in the rearward, now called for their horses to be brought up from the baggage park. The 'prickers' now began their grisly work. The Dale was the gateway to the river and they now rode along it, cutting down fleeing Lancastrians as they went. At the river bank fugitives were running upstream and downstream to find suitable fording places, and the riders wheeled along the banks to catch all they could. Some Lancastrians waded into what might have seemed a reasonably small river, only to find it was deeper than it looked and to drown in the freezing water. Where there were fording places some were successful and reached the other bank, others were despatched as they tried to escape, while still others were trampled in the headlong rush. Some must have lost their footing and gone into deeper water to drown. Any Yorkist archers who still had strength and fresh supplies of arrows may well have gone up to the bank to pick off enemy soldiers. Away from the southern ridge, the trees of Castle Hill Wood and Renshaw Woods provided welcome cover for desperate men, though no doubt Yorkist soldiers probed these sanctuaries. Over to the east lay the Towton–Ferrybridge road and, beyond it, marshland. To even reach it entailed a headlong dash over open ground, a target for archers and horsemen. Others fled north towards Towton, and streamed towards the Old London Road, following

This view of Bloody Meadow looking up from the River Cock, clearly shows the steepness of the slopes down to the river. In the weather on the day of the battle these would have been doubly treacherous. (Photograph by Graham Turner)

it to the crossing place at the Cock. It is likely that a ford, rather than a bridge, existed at the time at the crossing point. Edward Hall describes the fugitives here but makes no mention of a bridge, instead noting the depth of the Cock despite its seemingly small size. As further down the river, this place too became choked with the dead in the panic to get away, falling on top of one another until they formed a causeway, recounted by local people to Hall. This was the place of the so-called 'Bridge of Bodies'. According to Hall the water flowing from here to join the Wharfe turned the latter red with blood. Some Lancastrians may have managed now to grab horses if their baggage park was situated around Towton. Fugitives streamed north from the battlefield and from Towton village, desperate to reach Tadcaster. Behind them came the vengeful Yorkists.

All along the way between Towton and Tadcaster was a scene of slaughter as Yorkists harried the enemy, taking advantage of the easy targets presented by running foes. Many of the latter had thrown down their weapons and snatched off helmets to allow them to run more swiftly and to get more air. Their naked heads were a prime target for the roving horsemen. If they thought the River Cock was an obstacle, they now had to cross the Wharfe. Sources say the bridge had been broken by the Lancastrian army as it crossed from Tadcaster on 28 March. This seems a strange situation, suggesting that either it was not up to the weight of thousands of armoured bodies filing across it, or else it was deliberately destroyed by order of the commander. Why anyone would order the removal of a major escape route makes no sense at all. It may be that it was the Lancastrian leaders who in fact destroyed it after the battle, to block the route to the king in York, thereby trapping their own followers who had not yet passed over it. It may also have collapsed under the weight of fleeing Lancastrian soldiers. Whatever the truth of the matter, many resorted to attempting to cross the Wharfe itself, and drowned in such an attempt, adding significantly to the death toll. George Neville's letter to Coppini says that the Wharfe saw many drownings, and does not even mention the River Cock. Those who managed to reach the town were hounded in the streets by Yorkists and cut down when safety seemed so near. According to the Croyland chronicler the Lancastrians were hounded for ten miles as far as the gates of York itself. In the city there was panic as King Henry, Queen Margaret and their son made hasty plans to leave.

As the Yorkist prickers and other mounted men chased excitedly after the fleeing Lancastrians, Edward, according to the Croyland chronicler, stayed on the battlefield to await the return of his men. It was a wise move. He needed to be sure there would be no regrouping by dispirited enemies, and there had to be a secure base to which his soldiers could return after the pursuit. Edward did not want the army to fracture into small groups as darkness approached in hostile countryside. Moreover, most would be tired out after the prolonged and harrowing experience they had just been through, and only the adrenalin caused by blood lust, or the thought of stripping valuables or equipment from the dead and wounded, would keep them going. Commines reported Edward telling him that when victorious in battle he always mounted his horse and shouted orders to spare the commons but kill the lords. Edward would soon be told by heralds that, so far, a number of Lancastrian lords

THE ROUT (pages 74–75)

The Lancastrian line having broken, men flooded away from the battlefield at Towton. Many Lancastrians left the battle lines in the vicinity of Bloody Meadow (1), on the ridge at the rear or fled along the valley in the area known as Towton Dale (2), which afforded the easiest access to the River Cock (behind the viewer). As the Lancastrian battle lines finally crumbled, victorious Yorkist commanders launched mounted 'pricker's (3) at their dejected adversaries. These were horsemen who had largely remained in rear of the divisions, probably in the reserves. Less heavily clad than fully armoured knights and squires, their task was to use their lances to dissuade potential deserters, but also to chase the enemy if he broke and ran. Many of the men-at-arms, like the mounted archers, had dismounted to fight in the actual battle. With the day now won, some called for their horses to be brought up from the rear, so they could join in the chase. One such, wearing west European plate armour (4), now charges down on his prey, a retainer wearing the crescent badge of the Earl of Northumberland (5), who is dispatched with the beak of a horseman's hammer. In contrast to it's rider, the horse has little to protect it except a steel shaffron

for the top of it's head, whilst the man-at-arms also has saddle steels protecting the pommel and cantle of his saddle. The rider to the left wears a brigandine faced with blue velvet instead of a solid plate cuirass, but still has mail over steel vambraces to guard his arms (6). Unlike the other horseman he has no *bevor* to protect his chin, which is less constricting but leaves the upper throat more vulnerable. His saddle of wood has no steel facings. Of the men in the foreground, two in the centre wear padded jacks (7) and one on the far left a brigandine over his jack (8). The figure in the left foreground has managed to obtain a cuirass and *fauld* but has only mail over the shoulders and no protection on his arms (9). Three of the foreground figures wear *sallets*, one visored. That on the far right displays the rivets that secured an internal leather strip to which the padded lining was secured (10). Some have thrown away their helmets, the chin strap and weight on the head giving a feeling of encumbrance in their panic (11). In the middle distance a retainer of the Duke of Somerset, with his portcullis badge (12), has turned to fight and now stands at bay. The rider bearing down on him wears a kettle hat, an open helmet with a wide brim all round (13). (Graham Turner)

Chapel Hill seen from the Old London Road through Towton. In 1483 Richard III ordered the building of a chapel here, but it appears not to have been completed until about 1502, though after a grant of 1511 most records assert that it was never finished. By the time Drake wrote in 1736, the chapel had vanished. Towton Hall, where the mass grave was found, lies to the left of the site of the chapel.

appeared to have cheated death, unless they had been caught as they fled to the north of the field. The Duke of Somerset, having mounted as things became dangerously unstable, had galloped away northward, and many men of rank would try to do the same.

Even so, the death toll amongst the leading Lancastrians was high. The Earl of Northumberland had either been killed in the fighting or else pulled from the press to die from his wounds. Lord Dacre is said to have been killed by an arrow when he took off his helmet to drink during the battle. 'Lord Dacre's Bur Tree' was traditionally the site from which a Yorkist archer finished off the nobleman. The tree survived until the 19th century, and the site is within what is generally thought to be the Yorkist position. However, there must have been a number of such trees on the field, and how anyone could note one archer among many finishing off a particular lord is intriguing. Why a longbowman would try

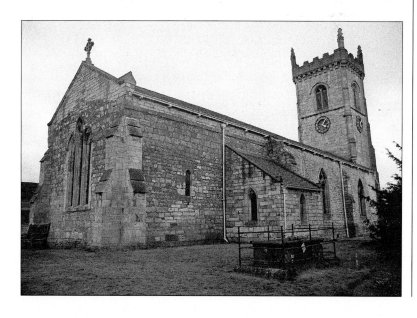

The tomb of Lord Dacre in Saxton churchyard. Damaged over the centuries, it now lies behind iron railings. Lord Dacre is said to have been discovered standing upright when the tomb was opened, and latterly his war-horse was found close by. Villagers probably took refuge in the church during the battle.

Harlech Castle, which held out against Lord Herbert and his Yorkists when other castles yielded.

to shoot while balancing in the branches is another point of discussion. It may simply have been a stray arrow, or at any rate one shot from the Yorkist side, that did the deed. Many noblemen wore no heraldic tabard at this time, and so it would necessitate an archer picking out the best-quality armour beneath a banner in the hope that there stood the noble himself. The incident nonetheless highlights the drawback of full armour, that the wearer becomes very hot and starts to dehydrate. In trying to alleviate this situation, Lord Dacre paid the ultimate price, in the same way perhaps as had Lord Clifford on the previous day. Lord Dacre was subsequently buried in a tomb in the churchyard of Saxton. The same churchyard was used to inter numbers of dead soldiers in trenches dug to the north side of the church, which can still be traced on the ground today. According to Leland in the 16th century, a member of the Hungate family, who owned the manor in Saxton, found bones on the battlefield that were presumably turned up from shallow graves when the fields were extended. These too were buried in the churchyard. One or other of these collections of bones were discovered in 1804 by workmen digging in the churchyard. Leland says that the Earl of Westmorland (a mistake by Leland for Westmorland's brother, John Neville) was also buried in the churchyard, the story received from those in Saxton he spoke with in 1585. No grave can be recognised today.

AFTERMATH

By any standards, in terms of lives lost, Towton was one of the costliest battles fought in Britain. As with other actions in the Wars of the Roses, the casualty list amongst the nobility was high. Of other men, the figures produced by the chroniclers are, as usual, dramatic. William of Salisbury's letter mentions 28,000 dead, not counting the wounded and those drowned, and, as if to stamp authority on the report, adds that this was the number recorded by the heralds. One duty of a herald was to wander the field after a battle and record the names of the fallen, often derived from their heraldic arms. If, as was common by this date, no tabard was worn by a lord, then presumably details were sought from his retainers. However, many of the soldiers that perished at Towton were not lords; they were ordinary billmen and archers, men who ran and were hacked down. As Boardman has noted, the dead must have included a large number of the soldiers raised by commissions of array. Did the heralds carefully note all these people spread over the distance from Saxton to Tadcaster, not to mention those piled in heaps in the River Cock or lost in the Wharfe? It seems right to deduce that, on this occasion, the 28,000 quoted included a large amount of guesswork, even if it was reported correctly in the first place.

Norham Castle on the border of Scotland. It was besieged in early June 1461 but relief forces chased off the Scots and Lancastrian attackers.

Unfortunately, the others chroniclers seem to have used this figure in their own reports, as it crops up several times. William Paston's letter to his brother, John, mentions 28,000 dead with a note about the heralds' report, while the Bishop of Elpin has the figure of 28,000, of which 800 were Yorkists. *Hearne's Fragment* puts the figure at 33,000 and the *Croyland Chronicle* makes the total 38,000, not counting those who drowned in the Wharfe. Fabian says 30,000 and Hall gives a rather exact figure over three days of 36,776.

So how many did in fact die? We shall never know. Many historians today do not believe that even the figure of 28,000 is acceptable. If a third of the army was destroyed it would be a grievous blow, and if an estimate of 25,000 is taken for the numbers that made up the Lancastrian army, then perhaps some 8,000 or more perished. The number of Yorkist dead was obviously less, and occurred not so much in the rout but rather during the battle as their ranks were pushed back; this figure may have been as many as 5,000. This would make a total of somewhere around 13,000 men killed; in itself a formidable figure – a great field of slaughter.

The Earl of Northumberland either died on the battlefield, as some chroniclers relate, or else was taken severely wounded to York, to die there. His body, with that of his brother, Sir Richard, was buried in the vault in the parish church of the Percy family in York, St Denis in Walmgate opposite their palace, though the Earl's tomb and effigy no longer survive. Others certainly died on the field. Lords Dacre, Mauley, Welles and Willoughby perished, along with Andrew Trollope. Lord Dacre now rests in Saxton churchyard. The body of Lord Welles was taken up by his family and conveyed to Methley, West Yorkshire (home of his first wife), where he lies buried in the family chapel in St Oswald's church, in a splendid alabaster tomb adorned with a military effigy. Edward's Act of Attainder lists the knights slain at Towton, though confusingly a few of them appear in later documents of the wars. William Gregory recounts that 42 Lancastrian knights were executed after the battle. On the Yorkist side, John Stafford and Horne of Kent perished, while Lord Scrope was badly injured.

Pembroke Castle remained in Lancastrian hands after Towton. Jasper Tudor, Earl of Pembroke, had much influence in west Wales but William Herbert moved against this opposition. He besieged Pembroke which, despite ample supplies and men, surrendered to him on 30 September 1461.

On the battlefield the mass of dead bodies needed to be interred. Some lay in heaps, some scattered about the field, many covered or partially covered in snow; the hard, cold ground and snow would make the job of the diggers very difficult. However, the *Croyland Chronicle* suggests that a thaw now set in, for it describes the snow beginning to melt and the blood and water mingled together, running in rivulets in the furrows. It may well have been at this time, therefore, that the River Cock was in spate, rather than during the battle. Before departing for York, Edward paid those who had the grisly task of bringing and burying the great number of corpses, 'piled up in pits and in trenches prepared for the purpose'. Wounded soldiers lying out in the fields were in imminent danger of dying from exposure. For some, the bitter cold may have helped slow the blood loss until they were tended. Many might find a quick death at the end of a knife as the battlefield was looted for arms, armour, jewels or other items, or vindictive soldiers saw an opportunity to kill yet another enemy. We know from the grave pits that wounds could be treated well and might heal without infection. With such a massive casualty list, however, the lottery of who received treatment probably meant many dying who might have been saved. Only the richest men could be guaranteed treatment from surgeons in their train. Edward, who of all people would have access to this, ironically seems to have escaped injury, but not through avoiding personal combat. Even with his household men around him, there is no doubt he had fought with great courage and had inspired his troops.

As news of the disaster reached York, Henry, Margaret and Prince Edward left the city and fled northwards at midnight. According to the *Brut Chronicle*, the Duke of Somerset, Lord Roos and others were in the city and left with them. On 30 March Edward entered York. The Earl of Devon (who, says *Gregory's Chronicle*, was sick in York) and three others were, according to Hall, executed and their heads replaced those of Edward's father and brother over Micklegate Bar. Henry and Margaret made for Scotland, and by 25 April they had negotiated for the regent, Mary of Guelders, to supply military assistance to their cause in return for handing over Berwick to the Scots. Edward tried both to placate Scotland and simultaneously to instigate unrest there.

Edward created his young brother, George, Duke of Clarence and created his uncle, Viscount Bourchier, Earl of Essex. Fauconberg was made Earl of Kent; several knights, such as Devereux, Herbert and Wenlock, became lords, and several squires and gentlemen became knights, including William Hastings and Humphrey Stafford. Edward's standard bearer, Ralph Vestynden, was rewarded the same year with an annuity of £10. The Earl of Warwick received little; already an extremely powerful man, he was in any case soon to fall out with Edward over the influence of the king's new relatives, the Woodvilles.

Edward entered York in triumph, and stayed for three weeks with no apparent desire to move on. For one thing his men badly needed time to rest and recover, and the wounded needed tending. He finally moved north to Durham, where he arrived on 22 April. Here he tried to obtain the loyalty of Bishop Lawrence Booth, a friend of Queen Margaret, making him his confessor. Proceeding to Newcastle, he witnessed the execution of James Butler, Duke of Ormond and Wiltshire, implacable foe of Richard of York. The head was sent down to London to be impaled

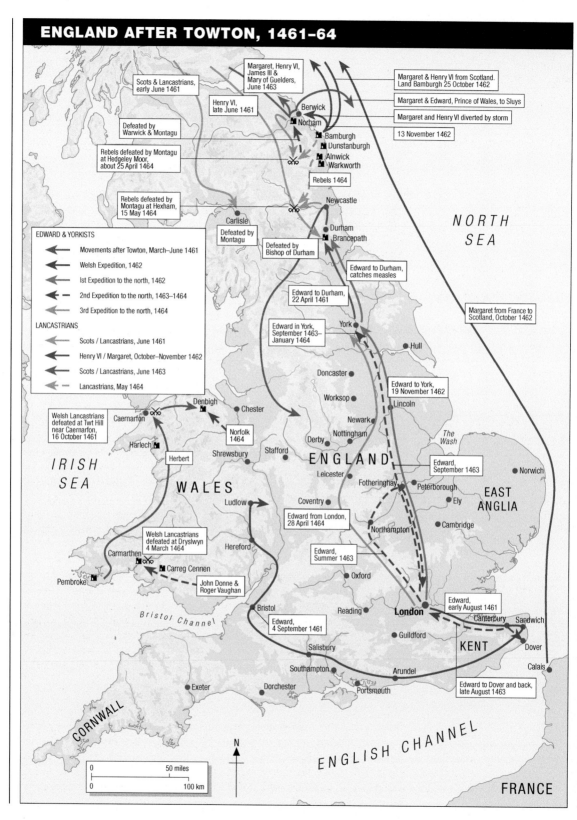

Scots & Lancastrians, early June 1461

Margaret, Henry VI, James III & Mary of Guelders, June 1463

Margaret & Henry VI from Scotland. Land Bamburgh 25 October 1462

Henry VI, late June 1461

Margaret & Edward, Prince of Wales, to Sluys

Margaret and Henry VI diverted by storm

Defeated by Warwick & Montagu

13 November 1462

Rebels defeated by Montagu at Hedgeley Moor, about 25 April 1464

Berwick

Norham

Bamburgh

Dunstanburgh

Alnwick

Warkworth

Rebels 1464

Rebels defeated by Montagu at Hexham, 15 May 1464

Newcastle

NORTH SEA

Carlisle

Durham

Brancepath

Defeated by Montagu

Defeated by Bishop of Durham

Edward to Durham, catches measles

EDWARD & YORKISTS

Movements after Towton, March–June 1461

Welsh Expedition, 1462

1st Expedition to the north, 1462

2nd Expedition to the north, 1463–1464

3rd Expedition to the north, 1464

LANCASTRIANS

Scots / Lancastrians, June 1461

Henry VI / Margaret, October–November 1462

Scots / Lancastrians, June 1463

Lancastrians, May 1464

Edward to Durham, 22 April 1461

Edward in York, September 1463–January 1464

York

Hull

Margaret from France to Scotland, October 1462

Doncaster

Worksop

Edward to York, 19 November 1462

Lincoln

The Wash

Denbigh

Chester

Newark

Nottingham

Welsh Lancastrians defeated at Twt Hill near Caernarfon, 16 October 1461

Caernarfon

Norfolk 1464

Derby

Harlech

Herbert

Shrewsbury

Stafford

E N G L A N D

Leicester

Edward, September 1463

Norwich

IRISH SEA

W A L E S

Ludlow

Coventry

Fotheringhay

Peterborough

EAST ANGLIA

Ely

Cambridge

Edward from London, 28 April 1464

Northampton

Welsh Lancastrians defeated at Dryslwyn 4 March 1464

Carmarthen

Hereford

Edward, Summer 1463

Carreg Cennen

Oxford

Pembroke

John Donne & Roger Vaughan

Bristol

Reading

London

Edward, early August 1461

Bristol Channel

Edward, 4 September 1461

Canterbury

Sandwich

Guildford

KENT

Dover

Salisbury

Calais

Southampton

Arundel

Portsmouth

Edward to Dover and back, late August 1463

Exeter

Dorchester

C O R N W A L L

N

E N G L I S H   C H A N N E L

FRANCE

| 0 | | 50 miles |
| 0 | | 100 km |

Warkworth Castle, from where Richard, Earl of Warwick conducted his offensive against the Lancastrian threat in Northumberland.

over London Bridge. Thence Edward moved westwards into Lancashire and Cheshire, before descending on the north Midlands, in a bid to win over areas strong in Lancastrian sympathisers. There was little resistance. Towton had broken the Lancastrians and cut a swathe through the ranks of their ruling elite. Edward was happy to welcome those who showed some contrition. Nevertheless, he may be considered rather too lax in the organisation he left in the north. Garrisons at Tynemouth and Newcastle were expected to control the northern borders; York was still largely Lancastrian in its sympathies. Edward simply left the Nevilles to sort out Northumberland and took his army away with him, missing the opportunity to assert authority in the region. In early June a force descended on Carlisle, to be beaten off by the arrival of John Neville, Lord Montagu. In late June King Henry was taken by Lords Roos, Dacre and Rougemont-Grey on a journey down to Brancepeth Castle in County Durham, in the hope of stirring revolt. They were chased off by the Bishop of Durham. Edward reached his manor of Sheen on 1 June and remained there until Friday 26 June, when he rode out and entered London. Two days later he was crowned in Westminster Abbey.

On 31 July the Earl of Warwick was appointed to the wardenship of the East and West Marches along the northern border with Scotland. This soon resulted in the capitulation of Alnwick and then Dunstanburgh castles. Meanwhile, in July, William Herbert and Lord Devereux had been ordered to raise troops against threats from Lancastrian supporters in Wales. Preparations for raising a fleet were put in train, and Yorkists in Wales advised to set themselves on a war footing. Edward made what was in effect a royal progress towards the area, by way of Canterbury, Sandwich, Arundel and Salisbury, arriving in Bristol on 4 September. However, he then moved to Ludlow before returning to London for the opening of parliament, leaving his lieutenants in Wales to carry on with the job. Herbert obtained the surrender of Pembroke Castle on 30 September, then defeated Jasper Tudor, the Duke of Exeter and Welsh Lancastrians at Twt Hill near Caernarfon on 16 October. In January 1462 Denbigh Castle capitulated, but in the west Carreg Cennan Castle remained a symbol of resistance, holding out until May, while Harlech Castle proved too tough a nut for Lord Herbert to crack.

In Scotland Edward's scheming resulted in raids by his sympathisers, while Warwick raided from the south. This led to a truce, allowing the border to be strengthened and Alnwick, which had been lost to the Lancastrians again in the winter of 1461/62, to be retaken. However, Margaret of Anjou now sailed to France to secure assistance. This was dogged by disagreement between her kinsman, Louis XI, and the Duke of Burgundy, who favoured the Yorkists. By the time she returned to Scotland she had obtained only 800 men. With her husband in tow, she landed near Bamburgh on 25 October 1462. The castle, together with those of Alnwick and Dunstanburgh, soon yielded. Edward called out nearly all the baronage, including two dukes, seven earls and 31 barons, while Warwick actively raised troops in the north. Margaret and Henry, disillusioned by the lacklustre support (probably partly caused by her making alliances with the Scots), took to the ships. The fleet was scattered by storms, and though the royal couple landed at Berwick, many Frenchmen came ashore at Lindisfarne, to be beaten by Yorkists. Edward had now reached Durham, where he caught measles. However, the Earl of Warwick conducted the sieges of Bamburgh, Alnwick and Dunstanburgh from his base at Warkworth. Blockaded, with men now eating their horses, only Alnwick had not offered to surrender by Christmas Eve. A relief force caused Warwick to pull back and the defenders marched out and off to Scotland. In early 1463 Edward came south to Fotheringhay, only to find himself betrayed in the north and the three castles again lost to him. More unrest followed, and though Warwick marched north he soon decided to call for Edward as well. Henry, Margaret, the young James III of Scotland and Mary of Guelders had come across the Border in June and in early July besieged Norham Castle on the River Tweed. Whilst Edward was at Northampton, Warwick, Montagu and the Archbishop of York had opposed the invaders, who panicked. Meanwhile Edward arrived at York, having sent out summonses, but did not press an attack on the castles or into Scotland, probably because of expense. On 9 December a truce was agreed with Scotland. However, discontent with the Yorkist government's expenses for a war that did not materialise was fomenting disquiet that needed quelling, and in the first months of 1464 Edward was busy to this end. Similarly in Wales trouble was brewing. The Duke of Somerset was stirring up unrest and the Duke of Norfolk was despatched to Denbighshire to deal with the situation. In South Wales, John Donne and Roger Vaughan routed the Lancastrians at Dryslwyn near Carmarthen.

Somerset made for Newcastle, hoping to find supporters now in the Yorkist garrison, but he had to flee in his nightshirt when recognised at Durham. He arrived at Bamburgh and from there led raids that included the seizure of Norham Castle. In April Montagu was sent north to escort the Scottish ambassadors. Avoiding an ambush near Newcastle, he was then attacked on about 25 April at Hedgeley Moor, nine miles from Alnwick. The Lancastrians were routed and one of the leaders, Sir Ralph Percy, killed. Montagu met the Scots at Norham and escorted them to York.

Edward left London on 28 March in order to besiege the Northumbrian castles, stopping to marry Elizabeth Woodville in secret on the way (1 May 1464). He then moved to Leicester for the muster. The rebel Lancastrians in the north, meanwhile, had come south from Alnwick and had reached the Linnels, a meadow some two miles from Hexham. Hearing of this, Montagu left Newcastle with speed, marched the 20 miles and fell on the rebel camp on 15 May 1464. Almost all the leading nobles were killed or captured soon afterwards, including Somerset, executed the same day. The Earl of Kyme, Lords Roos and Hungerford, and Sir Thomas Fynderne were caught a few days later and taken to Newcastle to be beheaded. Twelve knights and gentlemen were conveyed to York and executed. Alnwick and Dunstanburgh now opened their gates as Montagu advanced. Bamburgh refused, and was bombarded into surrender with siege guns at the end of June. Sir Ralf Grey, governor of Bamburgh, was taken to Doncaster and beheaded. Henry VI, at Bywell Castle, fled to the Pennines, and was finally captured the following year in a wood in Lancashire by William Cantlow. Edward, from York, agreed a 15-year truce with the Scots envoys.

Lancastrian resistance had, for the immediate future, been overcome. King Henry was transferred to London, his legs apparently bound to the stirrups of his horse. Once there he was taken to the Tower and into his final captivity. This gentle, rather simple man, would be put to death within the Tower in 1471. Edward was, for the moment, undisputed King of England.

THE GRAVE PITS

Something that makes the battle of Towton stand out amongst medieval battles is the fact that we are able to gaze upon a few of the soldiers who took part in the fighting. In 1996 part of a mass grave was discovered while digging the foundations for a garage at Towton Hall, which stands just west of the village itself, on the south side of the Old London Road, and next to the site of the later chapel. Following the discovery, an archaeological excavation was carried out on the site and 51 skeletons were found, resting in layers on top of each other in a rectangular pit some 3.25 x 2m in area and some 0.65m deep. The pit appeared to extend under the chimneybreast of Towton Hall. The skeletons were analysed by a team from the University of Bradford and West Yorkshire Archaeology Service.

It was soon discovered that the occupants had died violently. All were male, and it seems fairly safe to assume that they had taken part in the battle itself. Apart from earlier pot sherds few articles were found with the skeletons, the main items being copper-alloy 'aiglets' (the tips of the laces called points) used to fasten clothing or pieces of armour. One other piece may have been a fastener for armour.

The men ranged in height from 158.5cm (5ft 2½in) to 183.5cm (6ft), with an average height of 171.6cm (5ft 8in). Their ages ranged from youths of perhaps 16 to men over 50 years old (also the tallest), with no great bias to any one area. Two of the tall older men had previously healed wounds, suggesting that these were perhaps retainers, or else certainly recruits to the commissions of array, who had answered the call before. Tall men were often preferred for a lord's retainers, and are specified in summonses sent out to call up troops.

Three of the skeletons had variations in the bones of the arms and shoulders commensurate with that associated with modern longbowmen, and it is reasonable to suggest that these men too were archers. Others showed that their upper areas had from boyhood been involved in strenuous physical activity, though whether in military or farm work is

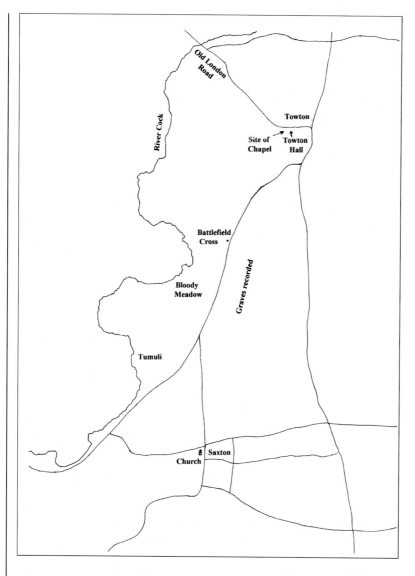

Areas of possible grave sites. Towton Hall has yielded a grave pit, though a virtual wall of bones was recorded earlier, while many others were found in graves around here and Chapel Hill. One record in 1736 in this area recalls five groats of the reigns of Henry IV, V and VII plus arrow piles and fragments of sword. The tumuli remain to be confirmed as medieval burial sites, though may be of the Bronze Age. Bloody Meadow is recorded as having five pits in it (Leland 1558), now destroyed, though Richard Brook, writing between 1848 and 1856, notes irregular patches of wild dwarf rose here, the 'Towton Rose', now virtually extinct. Farming also destroyed pits to the east of the B1217 road further north of Bloody Meadow, an area known as 'The Graves', where deep trenches 19 x 32 yards were still visible in the 19th century. Bones were deposited in trenches north of Saxton church by Yorkists, while the Hungate family in the 16th century re-interred in the churchyard bones they found presumably in shallow battlefield graves. Bones from the Towton Hall grave pits recently analysed were also re-buried in the churchyard. Remains were also discovered at the corner of Dinting Dale in 1835.

obviously impossible to deduce, except perhaps for those with previously healed wounds. It is important to note that some individuals were not tall and robust, and were therefore unlikely to have been experienced either in the army or on the farm. Perhaps these were men drawn from areas where no other suitable candidates could be found to join the array.

There is no way of knowing on which side the men had fought, and the grave pit was situated about a mile from the area generally agreed to have been where the main battle took place. Moreover, many had suffered head injuries. It is possible, therefore, that most represent Lancastrians fleeing from the battle later in the day, when the Yorkists were chasing them from the field. The lack of head protection could well have been the result of men throwing away their helmets as they ran, to get more air to the head and to release what would feel like an encumbrance. It could also, of course, have been due to the loss of the helmet during combat, or because some men did not own one. There

Dunstanburgh Castle, on the cliff above the Northumbrian coast, changed hands several times. Seized by Margaret of Anjou in 1462, it was recaptured by the Earl of Warwick soon after.

were worrying score marks on the sides of one individual's head, as though the work of a knife, perhaps the shearing of ears done before final despatch as an act of cruelty on a hated foe, or after death as an insult.

Thirteen skeletons bore wounds to parts of the body other than the head. Almost half had received only one wound, the others two or three, but Number 41 had received nine injuries, largely to the neck, arms and shoulder, as well as extensive head injuries. Other unassociated skeletal remains also showed injuries. Generally, most wounds to the torso and limbs were inflicted by edged weapons, far fewer being the work of concussive weapons. The largest group of wounds affected the arms and hands, and it was weapons such as the mace that were most likely to break a bone, whilst edged weapons were more likely to score it instead. The right ulna (in the forearm) was the bone most commonly affected, possibly the result of damage to the arm holding a weapon as it made to strike an opponent, or tried to ward off his blow. Cuts to the left side of the neck and collarbone are in keeping with a soldier facing a right-handed opponent. Other wounds to the back of the neck are more likely to have been inflicted when the man was running or perhaps lying face down. There are no rib wounds present, suggesting that body armour was being worn, or that such wounds missed the ribs and entered soft tissue only. It is unknown, of course, how many also suffered wounds involving soft tissue, as this leaves no trace in the skeletal record. Thus wounds to the abdomen, which would cause the contents of the digestive tract to infect the surrounding areas and almost certainly result in peritonitis and death, are unrecorded, as are those which reached the lung without scoring the ribs. It is also likely that weapons were aimed more at the head and limbs, especially the former, where a blow can either cause serious injury or debilitate sufficiently to leave the victim vulnerable to further attack.

Head injuries were present on all but one of the 28 skulls able to be analysed. Nine had already been wounded in the head before their final battle at Towton, and all these were well-healed injuries, with the number of previously healed wounds on an individual skull ranging from one to five – the latter perhaps an astonishing number for a man who then

Alnwick Castle. Lost to the Yorkists in September 1461, it was taken by Margaret of Anjou the following year. When Warwick besieged it he was threatened on 5 January 1463 by the Earl of Angus, which allowed the garrison under Lord Hungerford to march out.

fought again at Towton. Number 16 excites particular comment for the clear violence of an earlier, healed, wound. A blow had taken out a piece of bone from the left side of his lower jaw and also fractured it. Despite his luck (if it might be so called) in surviving this, he received no less than eight injuries of all types to his head at Towton.

Only one of the skulls analysed bore no head injury, the individual having been struck in the body instead. Of the others, the number of wounds received at Towton ranged from one to an extreme of 13, though about four wounds or less was average. The majority, 65 per cent, were blade wounds. Most were delivered from either the front or the rear, with a slight bias to the former. Over half had landed on the front or (recipient's) left side of the skull, suggesting that the two antagonists faced one another. Another 32 per cent were on the lower back of the head. The blade injuries vary in severity, from light wounds caused by the blade skidding over the surface, to deep cuts that bit right through the bone. Only 25 per cent of the head injuries were caused by blunt force trauma inflicted by concussive weapons. Of these most were to the lower jaw and left side of the head. Again, the spread of blows suggests that the majority came from the front or, to a lesser extent, the rear, and were delivered by right-handed assailants against the left side of the face. Unlike those wounds inflicted by edged weapons, over half of blunt force trauma wounds inflicted severe damage, breaking through the bone and causing portions of the skull to collapse. Such damage was presumably the work of percussion weapons such as the mace, rather than by any heavy weights pressing down on the skeleton in the grave. The third type of wound was a puncture wound, with eight skulls displaying a total of 12 of these. Half the wounds were to the rear of the skull and the rest to the sides. Three had been produced by stabbing with the tip of a blade, two producing triangular cuts caused by the blade being twisted as it was removed, thereby removing a small piece of bone, and one producing a diamond-shaped wound as made by the point of a thrusting sword. The other wounds are evidenced by four-sided entry wounds caused by the beaks or spikes of staff weapons or hammers. One individual, Number 41, had three such wounds, and must have been on the ground when he received at least the final two blows. The first would have felled him in any case, if not another of the multiple wounds he had received. Some punctures were of a form possibly suggesting the work of crossbow bolts with their four-sided heads, while slimmer examples were almost certainly delivered by the heads of armour-piercing arrows. On the left frontal bone of Number 40 was a wound made by a bodkin that had penetrated up to its skirt, while a general-purpose or barbed head had made a small penetration on the back of the head of Number 21.

The wounds could be categorised according to their type. Cuts to the bone were the work of swords or the blades of pollaxes or other staff weapons. Some cuts were short but some were notable in size; Number 6 showed a wound that produced a massive semicircular cut to the rear of the skull, while Number 25 had received a blow that sheared diagonally across the face to cut into the eye socket, nose and jaw.

Many wounds to the skull had been delivered by a right-handed opponent facing the receiver, as would be expected in combat. Others, however, had been delivered from behind and above, strongly suggesting that these were the result of mounted men slashing at fleeing opponents.

Shannon A. Novak made the point that if graves had been discovered nearer the centre of fighting, then more wounds, such as those from missiles, might have come to light. The large number of head wounds is surprising. The explanation that men threw away their helmets as they ran is an attractive one, especially as the graves were found in an area covered by the rout. However, it does not explain those frontal injuries to the head caused when face-to-face with an assailant. Perhaps they turned to face their pursuers.

Considering the large numbers of casualties that occurred at Towton, regardless of the exact number and whether or not the chroniclers were accurate, it seems highly likely that other grave pits were dug in the area. Several such have been noted in the past. A group was marked on maps in the area around Bloody Meadow and the Graves, others mentioned in documents. However, consistent ploughing of the agricultural land or other work has gradually destroyed any trace of these sites, though Veronica Fiorato thinks other graves may have survived below ground. There is another group of possible pits east of the River Cock and Castle Hill Wood, where three (possibly four) mounds survive. However, initial excavation of two of these to a depth of 0.61m in 1992 by the Towton Battlefield Society has failed to reveal any traces, and Veronica Fiorato has suggested that they configure to Bronze Age mounds rather than the more rectangular medieval examples. It should not be forgotten, of course, that large numbers were killed as they fled over the River Cock and streamed north towards Tadcaster. More perished trying to cross the River Wharfe, so there may well have been further pits at even greater distance from the site of the battle. The river itself may be the final resting place of many souls. It has recently been suggested that the excavated pit may have contained fugitives killed in and around Towton village, where their removal to a convenient mass grave was desirable. If lack of personnel to bury them meant the great majority were left where they fell, this may partly explain the paucity of grave sites. However, some do not believe the heralds would fail to organise burials.

The skeletons demonstrate precisely the damage of which medieval weapons are capable, probably in many cases against partially unarmoured bodies. This is always a sobering experience, and echoes the horrendous wounds seen on the famous skeletons from the grave pits from the battle of Wisby in Gotland in 1356. The fact that arrows can punch through bone reinforces the visual record of contemporary manuscripts and shows, for those who care to look carefully, that flesh was cut through like butter as shafts buried themselves almost up to the fletchings in unprotected bodies. Such wounds inflicted on war-horses helps demonstrate that here was one reason why armoured riders frequently dismounted in battle. Secondly, multiple wounds and possible mutilation show the ferocity that is unleashed in a battle when adrenalin is pumping and comrades are falling. In the bitter climate of the time, with scores to settle, there was little charity shown to a wounded foe. The other item of note is that several of the skeletons exhibit previous wounds that had healed up. Here were men who in some cases had experienced the horrors of close combat and suffered for it, yet had faced the same agonies again on that freezing, bleak field on Palm Sunday.

THE BATTLEFIELD TODAY

The field of Towton has not changed greatly from the day the battle was fought. No significant building work has encroached on the windswept open land, which remains strangely atmospheric. The roads are now metalled and the villages of Towton and Saxton have expanded over the centuries, but not overly so.

A tour might start at Ferrybridge, the site of the fierce engagement the day before the battle. The A1 now takes traffic over the river, but the early 19th-century bridge that replaced the older one still remains, close to where the modern dual carriageway thunders alongside the river. From the north side of the river the A162 turns off the A1 and heads north, through Sherburn-in-Elmet, where Edward may have made his main camp the evening before the battle. Further on is Barkstone Ash where, on the left of the road, still stands the stump of the cross plinth, the so-called 'Lepers Pot'. It is very likely that it was up this road that the Yorkists chased the retreating Lord Clifford. At Scarthingwell lies Dinting Dale, the presumed area where Clifford was finally killed. A left turn into Saxton Lane leads along Dinting Dale and into the village of Saxton. The church still stands, with the tomb of Lord Dacre on the south side of the churchyard. Taking a right turn up Cotchers Lane at the crossroads in Saxton village eventually leads to a T-junction with the B1217. Turning right on to it then leads towards Towton; it is this route that some say was the Old London Road, though more favoured is the A162 itself. By not turning into Cotchers Lane, the road from Saxton leads along Dam Lane to arrive at the B1217 further south, just above the deserted medieval village of Lead where stands the *Crooked Billet* public house. The church stands alone in the fields across from the road. This and the area around Saxton itself are probably where the Yorkist vanguard made camp.

The B1217 offers a number of views on its way to Towton. Around Lead church and just to the north, the River Cock runs quite close to, and roughly parallel with, the road. A little further up the B1217 a small country track opens on the left and eventually crosses the Cock. Before the bridge is reached, and once past the banked hedgerow on the right of the track, the view into the open field reveals a small tumulus with another beyond. The wood rising behind is Castle Hill Wood, where the supposed Lancastrian ambush party of 200 spears was stationed. Back on the main B1217 the road rises to the southern ridge and passes the western end of the initial Yorkist line approximately at the site of a small copse of trees by the roadside on the right. A little further on, a solitary tree far across the field on the right is the Hawthorn Tree and probably marks the forward edge of the vanguard of Yorkist archers. Castle Hill Wood is visible on the far left in a bulge in the river, which is hidden behind the steep slopes. A little further along on the same side is Bloody

Bamburgh Castle, perched on a cliff, refused to surrender to the Yorkists following the disaster at Hedgeley Moor in 1464 until cannon were brought into play and the place was bombarded into submission.

Meadow, with North Acres in the fields to the right of the road. This is the area between the two armies, and continuing north along the B1217 the main western edge of the Lancastrian line is reached, its rear approximately marked by the battlefield cross (Dacre's Cross) on the left side of the road. The cross usually has floral tributes laid on it. A path leads from the road into the fields beyond the cross. Here are Renshaw Woods, and from the gate, where stands an information panel, it is possible to see a wide sweep of the battlefield, with Bloody Meadow away in front and the fighting lines mainly across the B1217. Beyond the woods the steep slopes leading down to the Cock, bounded by trees and bushes, are now visible, though the area beyond the gate is private land.

Back on the B1217 the road continues north and joins the A162 just south of Towton village.

The A162 from Ferrybridge runs right across the eastern end of the battlefield and into Towton village. It then heads out of the village and runs northwards to join the A64 below Tadcaster, and thence to York. By turning left at the top end of Towton, past the *Rockingham Arms* public house, instead of following the A162 north, a road leads down through a farmyard. This is the route of the old London Road. On the left in the trees stands Towton Hall, where the mass grave was discovered in 1996. To the right of the hall is the grassy earthwork that is the presumed site of the lost chapel erected by Richard III. Ahead the road becomes a muddy bridle way through the fields. The track leads eventually down a steep incline to Cock Bridge over the river, which is probably one bottleneck that caused a disaster as fugitives tried to cross.

Other sites worth exploring are those in the immediate vicinity of the battle. Sandal Castle lies on the southern edge of Wakefield, and the earthworks and ruins are open to the public. The best view of the surrounding land may be obtained from the castle mound, with the river to the left and, to its right, the area where the battle of Wakefield is thought to have been fought, modern housing having been kept at bay to some extent. Pontefract Castle is now an extensive ruin but can be visited during opening hours.

A number of archaeological artefacts have come to light over the centuries. A battleaxe found in the valley of the River Cock was once owned by a miller at Saxton. Purchased from him by a Colonel Grant, it was presented to the Duke of Newcastle in 1854 and remains on display at Alnwick Castle. The shape suggests a side arm rather than a knightly weapon, though the haft is a replacement. A decorated spur was discovered in about 1792 and presented to the Society of Antiquaries of London. A gold ring with a lion on the bezel, presented to the same Society in 1786, is now in the British Museum. Another ring, silver gilt with conjoined hands, was given to a Dr Whittaker in 1816 but has since been lost. A narrow blade some 2ft 4¼in long but ½in wide, now also lost, was discovered in the 19th century but is more likely to have been a later small sword than a medieval weapon. A spearhead, now lost, was also reputedly found on the battlefield, appeared in a local blacksmith's shop in the 1840s, and was later bought from him. At this distance, of course, the provenance of some of the items cannot be proved, and the absence of others means they cannot be dated. Finds by the responsible use of metal detectors have revealed a variety of pieces, but the constant use of the area as farmland means that many others have probably been lost. Many precious items would have been looted from bodies when the battle ended, if not before, and it is no surprise that most are fittings or items of clothing, such as heraldic cast or engraved buttons. One intriguing item was the so-called 'Towton Dog-Collar'. Dug up around Saxton Grange Farm, it was used as a dog-collar until the owners noticed that the brass collar (if it was not gold) was encrusted with precious stones under the dirt. It sold in London in 1926 for £1,500 and disappeared from public view. Since it was made of many pieces and reportedly stretched when pulled, it may have been a nobleman's collar, perhaps a Lancastrian collar of SS, though this cannot be proven. The collar of SS was derived from a badge of Henry IV and worn by some Lancastrians of rank.

BIBLIOGRAPHY

Barber, Richard, *The Knight and Chivalry* (Longman Group Ltd., London, 1970)

Bellamy, J.G., *Bastard Feudalism and the Law*, (Routledge, London, 1989)

Blair, Claude, *European Armour* (B.T. Batsford Ltd, London, 1958)

Boardman, Andrew W., *The Medieval Soldier in the Wars of the Roses* (Sutton Publishing Ltd, Stroud, 1998)

Boardman, Andrew W., *The Battle of Towton* (Sutton Publishing Ltd, Stroud, new ed., 2000)

Bradbury, J., *The Medieval Archer* (The Boydell Press, Woodbridge, 1985)

Bradbury, J., *The Medieval Siege* (The Boydell Press, Woodbridge, 1992)

Brooke, Richard, 'The field of the battle of Towton', paper given before Society of Antiquaries, London, 1849

Brooke, Richard, Visits to fields of Battle in England (1857, repro facsimile Alan Sutton,Dursley, 1975)

Burgess, M., 'The Mail-Maker's Technique', *Antiquaries Journal* XXXIII pp. 193–202 (London, 1953)

Burne, A.H., *Battlefields of England* (Methuen & Co.,London, 1950)

Contamine, Philippe, *War in the Middle Ages*, (trans Jones, Michael), (Basil Blackwell Publisher Ltd, Oxford, 1984)

Cunnington, C. Willet and Phillis, *Handbook of English Mediaeval Costume* (Faber & Faber Ltd, London, 1969)

Curry, Anne, and Hughes, Michael, (ed.), *Arms, Armour and Fortifications in the Hundred Years War* (The Boydell Press, Woodbridge, 1994)

Davis, R.H.C., *The Medieval Warhorse* (Thames & Hudson Ltd, London, 1989)

Dufty, R., and Read, W., *European Armour in the Tower of London* (HMSO, London, 1968)

Edge, David, and Paddock, John Miles, *Arms and Armour of the Medieval Knight* (Bison Books Ltd, London, 1988)

Embleton, G., and Howe, J., *The Medieval Soldier* (Windrow & Greene Ltd., London, 1994)

Embleton, Gerry, *Medieval Military Costume* (The Crowood Press Ltd, Ramsbury, 2000)

Fiorato, Veronica, Boylston, Anthea, and Knüsel, Christopher, *Blood Red Roses. The Archaeology of a Mass Grave from the Battle of Towton AD 1461* (Oxbow Books, Oxford, 2000)

Foss, Michael, *Chivalry* (Michael Joseph Ltd, London, 1975)

Gies, Frances, *The Knight in History* (Robert Hale Ltd, London, 1986)

Gillingham, J., *The Wars of the Roses* (Weidenfeld & Nicolson, London, 1981)

Haigh, P.A., *The Military Campaigns of the Wars of the Roses* (Sutton Publishing Ltd., Stroud, 1995).

Haigh, P.A., *The Battle of Wakefield 1460* (Sutton Publishing Ltd., Stroud, 1996)

Hardy, Robert. *Longbow* (Mary Rose Trust, Portsmouth, 1976, 1992)

Keegan, J., *The Face of Battle* (Pimlico, London, 1991)

Keen, Maurice, *Chivalry* (Yale University Press, London, 1984)

Keen, Maurice, (ed.), *Medieval Warfare* (Oxford University Press, Oxford, 1999)

Koch, H.W., *Medieval Warfare* (Bison Books Ltd, London, 1978)

Lander, J.R., *The Wars of the Roses*, (Secker & Warburg, London, 1965)

Mann, Sir James, *Wallace Collection Catalogues. European Arms and Armour*, 2 vols (The Trustees of the Wallace Collection, London, 1962)

Markham, Sir Clement, 'The Battle of Towton', *Yorkshire Archaeological and Topographical Journal* (10, 1889)

Myers, R.A., *Household of Edward IV* (Manchester University Press, Manchester, 1959)

Nicholas, Sir Harris, *Wardrobe Accounts of Edward IV* (London, 1830)

Norman, A.V.B., *Wallace Collection Catalogues. European Arms and Armour Supplement* (The Trustees of the Wallace Collection, London, 1986)

Oakeshott, R. Ewart, *The Sword in the Age of Chivalry* (Lutterworth Press, London, 1964)

Pfaffenbichler, M., *Armourers* (British Museum Press, London, 1992)

Prestwich, M., *Armies and Warfare in the Middle Ages. The English Experience* (Yale University Press, London, 1996)

Ross, C., *The Wars of the Roses: A Concise History* (Thames & Hudson, London, 1976)

Seymour, William, *Battles in Britain* (Vol I) (Sidgewick & Jackson Ltd, 1975)

Smurthwaite, David, *The Ordnance Survey Complete Guide to the Battlefields of Britain* (Webb & Bower, London, 1984)

Starley, David, 'Metallurgical analysis of medieval quarrel heads and arrowheads', *Royal Armouries Yearbook*, Vol. 5 (2000, pp. 178–186)

Thompson, M.W., *The Decline of the Castle* (Cambridge, 1987)

Turnbull, Stephen, *The Book of the Medieval Knight* (London, 1985)

Original Sources

Calendar of State Papers and Manuscripts in the Archives and Collections of Milan, Vol. 1 (1385–1618), Hinds, A.B. (ed), (London, 1912)

Croyland Abbey Chronicle, Riley, H.T. (ed), (H.G. Bone, London, 1854)

Edward Hall's Chronicle, Ellis, H., (London, 1809)

'Hearne's Fragment', *Chronicles of the White Rose of York*, Giles, J.A. (ed), (London, 1834)

'The Rose of Rouen', *Archaeologia* 29 (1842, pp.343–7)

Vergil, Polydore, *Three Books of Polydore Vergil's 'English History', comprising the Reigns of Henry VI, Edward IV and Richard III, from an Early Translation, preserved among the Manuscripts of the Old Royal Library in the British Museum*, ed. Ellis, H. (Camden Society old series 29, 1844)

Worcester, William, *Annales Rerum Anglicarum*, ed. Stevenson, J. (B. White, London, 1864)

Medieval Prints and Cards
by

Graham Turner

Graham Turner's atmospheric painting 'The Battle of Towton' is available as a fine art print - part of a range of prints and cards reproduced from his work.

Other similarly evocative subjects include the battles of Bosworth, St. Albans, Barnet and Tewkesbury, together with more peaceful images inspired by this colourful chapter in our past.

For details of the complete range, ask for our **FREE COLOUR CATALOGUE -** 'The Historical Art of Graham Turner' - or visit the Studio 88 Web Site.

Details of all currently available original paintings by Graham Turner can also be found on the web-site - or contact Graham through Studio 88 for an up to date list.

Studio 88 LIMITED

P.O. Box 88, Chesham, Bucks. HP5 2SR

Phone & Fax: 01494 785193

info@studio88.co.uk

www.studio88.co.uk

INDEX

Figures in **bold** refer to illustrations